*"And we know that in all things
God works for the good of those who
love him."*

Romans 8:28 (NIV)

D1113819

WHEN EVIL STRIKES

The names of individuals and organizations and some of the details in this book have been disguised to protect both innocent and guilty. The names and incidents concerning the Herrod family are factual.

Copyright © 1992 by Lila Wold Shelburne

Published by HANNIBAL BOOKS,
a division of Hefley Communications,
HANNIBAL, MO 63401

ISBN 092-929-2251
LIBRARY OF CONGRESS NO. 92-071595

Printed in the United States of America
by Lithocolor Press, Inc.,
Second printing, August, 1992.
Cover design by Cyndi Allison
Book design by Marti Hefley / Mary Leah Christmas

"Scripture taken from the HOLY BIBLE, NEW INTERNATIONAL VERSION. Copyright © 1973, 1978, 1984 International Bible Society. Used by permission of Zondervan Bible Publishers."

DEDICATION

For my loving husband, Clayton,
and our children,
Shayne, Marthina and Sharmion,
for their confidence and encouragement

1982

I hate him. Hate. Hate. Hate him. So pious. So self-righteous. A man of God, they call him. Of course he serves God. Why should he not? He always wins; is always successful.

Dr. Ron Herrod, with his fine and growing ministry. He prospers in everything he does. If only I could catch him off guard. If I could tempt him when his defenses were lowered. I could then remove that smirk they call a smile. But he will have nothing to do with me. He remains loyal to his God.

Look at him with his beautiful wife and adoring children. Such a niiiice family. So haaappy. So full of jooooy. How I would like to destroy him and all the good he has done.

Ah! But what if I attacked him through this family he loves soooo much. That niiiiice family that sings and laughs and prays. Yesssss. That is where he is vulnerable. I will stalk his family until I find an opportunity to create a situation that will defeat them all. They will surely curse their God before I am through.

Where to strike? Who would be most susceptible? And what would be the plot? This diabolical scheme must have faaar reaching consequences ..."

Twila Herrod's short legs dangled from her perch on the kitchen stool. She was watching herself in a mirror as she practiced her very best eight-year-old smile for the family picture that was going to be taken. *I wonder if I look best with an open smile or a closed smile.* Every time she changed smiles she moved her head.

"Twila, please sit still or I'll never get the tangles out," her sister demanded.

"I'm trying, Dawn, but it's so exciting to get our pictures taken. Isn't it wonderful?"

"It's just for the church directory."

"But everybody will see our picture; I can't look terrible."

"I'm not going to let you look terrible, but you've got to sit still."

"But you keep pulling. It hurts."

"I'm not pulling it, you are. Every time you wiggle."

"You think you are so smart. Just 'cause you're fifteen."

"Hush, Twila. Stop your fussing and be thankful you've got a big sister who cares about how you look." The mother's calming voice was only slightly tinged with impatience as she entered the kitchen in her robe, grabbed a towel and wiped Twila's tears.

"Mommy, will my blue dress match yours and Dawn's okay for the picture?"

"Yes, Twila," Emily replied, "and the Peter Pan collar is very flattering. You will look fine. I'm going to wear my pink dress with the puffy sleeves. Now we've got to hurry or we'll be late. Try to sit still. And Dawn, remember, your sister never has had any pain tolerance."

"What's tolerance?" Twila demanded.

"It's the ability to put up with something," Dawn explained. "I'm tolerating you right now."

"Well, I don't tolerate pain. Ouch!"

"Let's make a deal. You sit still three more minutes and I won't hurt you. Not deliberately."

"Okay." Twila shut her eyes again and entered her own little dream world. *I like my daddy being the pastor of First Baptist Church of Kenner. I like the way it's growing. Before long it's going to be one of the biggest churches in New Orleans and by the time I grow up and get married it's going to be gigantic. And when I get married I'll have the biggest wedding ever and I'll wear a pure white wedding dress with lots and lots of lace and ribbons and ...*

"Now, let me get the part straight," Dawn said, gently drawing the comb across the top of Twila's head. Twila held her breath until Dawn had finished making the part.

Daddy can give me away and marry me. By then Dawn will have kids and maybe they can be my ring bearer and flower girl and, "Oh dear, my brother doesn't like going to weddings."

"Close your eyes while I spray it."

"Phew!" Twila fanned the air with her hands. "It sure takes a lot of work to get pretty, huh? Maybe I should cut my hair."

"Maybe, just don't go jumping around and getting all messed up."

"I won't, Dawn." Twila bounced down the hall to her parents' bedroom. "Mom, can I cut my hair?"

"You'd look like a boy if you did that, Knothead. Then I wouldn't be able to recognize you." Ron was slipping into his suit jacket.

"I wouldn't either look like a boy, Daddy. Besides, anybody can recognize a Herrod. We've all got your pointed nose and dark circles around our eyes. Miss Sally thinks Mommy collects raccoons because they remind her of you. Huh, Mommy?"

"Well, I have always liked raccoons," Emily admitted. "And yes, when she said that, I guessed she might be right."

"Is everyone ready?" she called while picking up her purse. "Where's Joey?"

"He's on the couch reading some book about starting his own business," Twila announced as she twirled around and around in the middle of the bedroom floor, and watched her skirt flare. "Dad, is that why you got Mom that raccoon plate?"

"I gave Mom the plate because I love her. Come on now, let's go." Twila ran to the car. "I get to sit by the door."

"Move it, kid." Joey ordered. The Herrod's only son felt that since he was five years older, he could exercise authority over his kid sister.

"Mommy, Joey won't let me sit by the door."

"Just move over, Twila. Please don't make a fuss."

"Yes, sir. But I'm still gonna get my hair cut." A warm smile flashed across her face. "Daddy, I could still wear bows if my hair were short." Twila continued her chatter. "Mommy, I've got our family all figured out."

"How's that, Sweetie?"

"You and me are alike 'cause we line our shoes up in our closets and we both have blonde hair and blue eyes and we both like to talk."

"You especially like to talk," her brother agreed.

"You do too, Joey. Besides, I didn't ask you. We all like to talk except Dawn and Daddy when he's home at night. That's how they are alike and both have brown hair and brown eyes."

"Brunettes, goofy." Joey, always half annoyed and half amused by his little sister, couldn't resist the friendly put-down. "People with dark eyes and hair and olive skin are called brunettes."

"I knew that."

"Yeah, sure. So what about me?"

"You're sorta half mom and half dad. I've decided brunettes are quiet people and blondes really do have more fun. Huh, Mommy?" Twila wasn't sure why everyone started laughing.

She watched her Dad reach over and squeeze her mom's hand and saw his eyes light up when he glanced her way. Twila liked what she saw and wiggled with joy. "Mommy, how long have you and Daddy been married?"

"Nineteen years."

Twila sighed deeply. *I'm going to be in love forever and my husband's going to buy me pretty clothes and rings and take me out to eat in beautiful places with tablecloths and candles and flowers.*

"Daddy, I'm hungry. Can we go to McDonald's after we get our pictures taken?"

For weeks Twila talked about cutting her hair. "I'm tired of long hair, Mom, I really do want it cut."

"How short do you want it?"

"Real short. Like this." Twila flattened her hand and chopped at the base of her head.

"That short? Twila, that's a hairline cut."

"I know. That's what I want."

"If you're sure ..."

"I'm sure. Can you cut it now?"

Emily looked at her watch. "Maybe, if we hurry."

"I'll get the scissors."

Twila sat uncharacteristically still while Emily cut the guideline. Then she asked, "Wouldn't it be nice for you and me to have lunch together, Mommy? We could just go to McDonald's." Twila turned and smiled hopefully.

"So, what's in the Happy Meal this time?"

"It's the last week to get the McDonaldland Express, and if you get one and I get one I'll have the full train. Please?"

"Well, I guess if you'll sit still so I can get done."

"Mom, will you tell Dad about my hair?"

"Why, Twila, this is your idea. You tell Dad."

"What if he gets mad?"

"He isn't going to get mad. He might be disappointed at first, but he won't be mad."

"But what will I say if he's disappointed?"

"Well now, Sweetie, there's something you need to learn about men ..."

That evening Ron found an envelope, addressed "Dad," in the center of his desk. Opening it, he found wads of long blonde hair.

The storm raged through Ft. Smith, Arkansas as suddenly as the death that claimed the life of Eugene Marrow's uncle three days earlier. Rain blew horizontally, slamming into the huddled group of mourners beside the yawning grave. The flapping awning overhead offered little protection to eleven-year-old Eugene who stood on the outer edge of the mourners. In minutes the clothes on his exposed side were wet to his skin. It was odd, feeling wet on one side, dry on the other.

Eugene's feelings these past three days were just as odd. He supposed he should feel sorrow because his mother's only brother was dead. Instead, Eugene felt a strange mix of guilt and relief. Almost a giddy relief, quiet and deep, which forced his head down and choked him to silence. Everyone assumed he was grieving.

"I know it's hard losing your favorite uncle," a neighbor consoled as he rumpled Eugene's hair. "I used to bowl with your Uncle George, Eugene, and one thing certain, he sure did love his Little League boys," comforted another. "It's all he ever talked about." Every hand that touched Eugene seemed only to stir the anger and hurt bottled inside him.

Eugene's father went off on another drinking binge while Eugene and his mother, Verna, went to Auntie Lou's house. For three days Eugene heard people talking about how great his Uncle George was and how poor Auntie Lou was alone now because they didn't have any children. Everybody knew George; he was the vice-president at the Fourth National Bank.

After a long, awkward silence, a man Eugene vaguely recognized said, "I never could get over how George would babysit for half the boys on his team." The jolting news brought a sudden wave of nausea that emptied Eugene's stomach into his throat. Horrified, he stumbled from the room.

Eugene hated what Uncle George had done every time he babysat him. It wasn't that George was mean. He didn't get mad and swear and make Eugene feel stupid. George talked nice and was patient. Eugene could still hear his uncle's favorite line. "If you really love me, you'll let me teach you the secrets of being a real man."

Then George would start touching him. "What do you suppose uncles are for?" George was always so nice. Eugene couldn't hurt his uncle's feelings by saying no. "We'll play your favorite games first, then we'll play some of mine." George always added a new game before he let Eugene go to sleep.

"But I don't like your games," Eugene had complained, and George would start laughing. They'd both laugh because George could make anything funny. Then he'd say, "I'll know when you're a real man because you'll start liking my games and you won't complain any more."

When George finally left the bedroom, Eugene would pull the covers over his head and cry. He felt confused, unable to understand why pleasing his uncle seemed so wrong and made him feel dirty. Eugene liked his Uncle George and they did have a lot of fun together. He wasn't mean like his dad.

Eugene remembered the way his father used to treat him when he was really little. The tickling would start out in fun. Eugene would titter and snicker at first, like any child who craves the camaraderie of a parent. Then, breathless and tired, little Eugene would gasp and plead, "No more, Daddy. Please. Stop, Daddy. Please stop." Sometimes he'd beg for his mom to intervene. "Mom, make Daddy stop," he'd cry. "Please, Mommy, please."

"You do, Verna, and you'll be sorry," Clyde would warn his wife. "It's time he learns to take a little teasing like a man. You wanna make a wimp out of him or something?" Verna would walk out of the room. Clyde's tormenting would continue until Eugene either vomited or wet himself.

"Why you little ..." Clyde would cursed violently. "Look what you did to me. Eugene would have to clean up the mess. Once the job was done, he never knew if he'd be treated to a drink of beer from his father's can or be spanked and sent to bed.

Since Eugene had grown big enough to avoid being tickled, his dad's favorite sport was lighting his cigarette and flipping the still burning matches at Eugene's bare arm or leg. The youngster learned to sneak off to his room early and study just to avoid his father.

Eugene had been too old for a sitter for the past couple of years. He'd learned a lot since those sessions with Uncle George. He now realized he had been betrayed, and he hated his uncle. Eugene felt guilty for being stupid enough to play his uncle's disgusting games, and he hated himself even more for being so gullible. The thought of George's false kindness and sickening demands made Eugene retch again and he spit the bitter taste from his mouth.

The only two men Eugene had ever really known were his uncle and his father. Still, he did not regret that George was dead.

J oAnn Watson basked in the solitude of her upstairs bedroom. From her window she could see a large rainbow stretched across Puget Sound. It was a familiar scene to the residents of Seattle, Washington and she wondered how long it would be before she'd see it again. In only two hours she would be Mrs. John Taylor of St. Louis, Missouri.

JoAnn's wedding dress reflected in the mirror behind her as she lifted strand after strand of her thick blonde hair, gripped each one briefly in her curling iron and then let the soft curl drop. As each lock fell, she thought of a goal achieved. For years she'd disciplined her life by setting goals.

Her ambition since childhood was to marry and have babies. Seven, she'd finally decided, would be the perfect number, and she pictured herself driving a station wagon, living in a comfortable suburban home and being the local Kool-Aid mom. "JoAnn, you'll have our blessings for marriage as soon as you finish college and get at least a year of work experience," her mother had said. The necessity of the groom being a strong Christian had long before been established.

Knowing her parents wouldn't budge, and respecting their opinions too highly to object, JoAnn took college classes between her last two years of high school and left for St. Louis University the fall after she graduated. She didn't give herself a break from studies until she'd completed her degree three years later.

In addition to her B.S., JoAnn had an engagement ring. She'd met John, a sophomore, the first semester of her freshman year in the college class of her church. A new friend, Donna Mills from Houston, Texas, introduced them. "John Taylor, meet JoAnn Watson, a freshman business marketing major."

It was the following year before John asked JoAnn for a date. Halfway into his senior year as a computer science major, he gave her a ring.

JoAnn took a last, quick look at herself in the full length mirror and was satisfied with her cascade of curls. The soft cloud of her fingertip veil felt like a benediction as it rested lightly against her face. Her long cathedral train seemed to symbolize the beautiful years to come.

The congregation stood as she started down the aisle. With her eyes fixed on John she anticipated their honeymoon in Hawaii, their return to St. Louis and their move into their own small condo. Most of all, she looked forward to the day she would bear their first child.

JoAnn smiled to herself as she anticipated the day she could waddle into work and resign. She would have no regrets at stepping off the ladder of success and leaving her $25,000-a-year management position in exchange for the challenge of being a full-time mother and homemaker.

"With this ring, I thee wed ... for better or worse ... until death do us part." JoAnn looked up into John's smiling face. She felt only peace about promising her life, as well as her heart, to the strong, quiet man she'd come to love.

1986

J oAnn, still groggy from surgery, placed her hand on the bandage that covered her incision. Dr. Meyers stood at the foot of her bed, scanning the pages in her chart. "Good morning, JoAnn. Looks like you're moving around pretty good."

"Is everything okay?"

"Yes, and as I said yesterday, there's no malignancy, but we didn't expect there to be. The tumor came out fine." Almost as an afterthought he added, "You might have trouble having babies."

You might have trouble having babies? The words flashed like huge red lights through the fog in JoAnn's mind. *You might have trouble having babies.* The words haunted JoAnn continually the two years following her surgery. They seared every time she saw a child in a store, or she held one in her church nursery.

Unlike many barren women, she never avoided others' babies. Instead, she filled her empty arms with the babies of her friends. She couldn't resist baby showers and she dreamed of the children she would someday have as she bought lavish gifts for her friends.

Several times she arranged to babysit. "Why don't you leave the baby with John and me?" she'd offer. "It's time you two enjoy a night out."

When she needed to talk, she'd call her mother. "Mom, my doctor wants to do another surgery." Living halfway across the continent never really separated JoAnn from her mother, Judy. They both used the phone freely when either wanted to visit. "There's a chance it might help. If it doesn't, we'll see an infertility specialist."

"Is it really that big a rush, JoAnn? You're young, you've got an excellent career, and the pay's wonderful. You have time to travel and save. Besides, who knows what might happen if you relax a bit ... "

"Do you have any idea how many people told us to relax before we went to the Bahamas last week? And how many said the same thing six months ago when we went to the Canary Islands? Mother, relaxing has nothing to do with conception. That idea belongs with all the other old wives' tales."

"Well, maybe, but you've always been in such a hurry to live life. Slow down and enjoy being young."

"But all I've ever wanted was to be a mother, and it's been four years now. I don't care about all this other stuff. Is that being impatient?"

"Not from your perspective, JoAnn, but one of these days you'll have your baby and we'll all be happy for you."

Aaaaugh! Four years of stalking and I still haven't devised the right ploy. How can I best humble this "humble servant?" Perhaps one of his daughters. Yesssssss. Daughters are always dear to a daddy's heart.

Hmmmmnn, what delicious options come to mind. I shall devise a delightful destruction that will go on and on and on and on. But which girl? It is disgusting the way both girls parrot their parents' faith in God.

Now to watch them. To seek out the perfect opportunity to ensnare one of them in a way that will not only destroy her life, but cause the whole family to doubt His "goodnesssssssss."

Twila gently shook her packages that sat under the tree, wishing she could know what each beautiful box contained but not really wanting to guess and ruin the surprise. With each added package, her anticipation mounted. One moment she acted like the young lady she was fast becoming, and the next, like the little girl she still was.

"Twila, aren't you going to finish frosting these cookies?"

"Yeah, but I had to take a break. The tree is so pretty. I think it's prettier every year," she said. "When is everybody coming tonight?" Twila almost floated back into the kitchen.

"Six-thirty. You're just able to appreciate the tree more each year, Twila, so it seems prettier. Oh, my!" Emily looked at her watch. "We do need to hurry or we won't be ready." She popped her last tray of Christmas tree cookies in the oven as Twila scooped up a knife loaded with green frosting.

"What's a phlegmatic?"

"Why do you ask?"

"Just something we were talking about in school."

"Oh. Well, it's a descriptive term for a laid back type of personality. I'm rather phlegmatic."

"Is Dad?"

"No. Although at home he appears that way because home is his relaxing place, but he's a choleric, hard driving, and goal oriented. He motivates people to get things done."

"Bossy like?"

"No, not bossy but he does assign responsibilities and he expects people to get things done. Some people refer to him as a 'type A' personality." Emily talked as she cleaned away her baking mess. "That's just another way of categorizing a type of personality."

"What am I?" Twila set a tray of frosted cookies aside and licked her fingers.

"Sanguine, life of the party, encourager. You have a positive outlook on life and you sorta naturally shrug off unpleasant things. But, you've a bit of Daddy's hard driving choleric, too."

"What about spiritual gifts?"

"Well now, Twila, that's entirely different. We're born with our personalities, but God gives us a spiritual gift when we become Christians." Emily poured a cup of coffee, added her half-and-half, took a cookie and sat down beside Twila.

"See, Twila, Daddy and I can be faced with the same situation and we'll respond entirely differently. Daddy's gift is prophesy and his immediate reaction is to identify and deal with the sin that caused the problem. Anything he perceives as sin really upsets him. Your mother's not so concerned with the cause as the solution, and that's typical of someone with my gifts of administration and organization."

"Is that why Dad always blows up?"

"Now, sweetheart, Daddy doesn't always blow up. He might let off a bit of steam now and then, and rightly so when you've disobeyed, but that's better than holding all his feelings in and getting a stomach ache, the way I tend to do. He just recognizes the problem for what it is, instead of calling it something else."

"So he identifies problems and you solve them?" Twila had finished her cookies and looked up at Emily.

"You might say that."

"Mom, I think you're burning the cookies."

Think you're smart, don't you. Think you're tough stuff, starting line and all." Instead of pride in his son's accomplishments, Clyde Marrow felt intimidated. He couldn't tolerate his son's success. Marrow's words, slurred from drinking, grew louder as he began to curse and exaggerate every wrong, real or imagined, Eugene had ever done.

This time Eugene didn't sit silently. "No, Dad, I don't think I'm smart." Eugene spoke calmly, matter-of-factly, but said exactly what he felt. "I've simply tried to do my best, and yes, I'm proud of my accomplishments. I thought you would be, too." Clyde raised his doubled fist and Eugene, for the first time in his life, didn't run. At sixteen, he couldn't beat his father but he returned blow for blow until the police arrived.

Clyde was taken into custody to sober up and, when released, he returned home only briefly. He sulked and talked only to Verna, then was gone. Over the months his visits came further apart, and a change came over Mrs. Marrow. Eugene could feel her antagonism as slowly in her heart she too abandoned him.

"If you'd have just kept your mouth shut, Eugene," she cried, "he'd still be here." Unknowingly, her words cut the last tie between them.

Spring 1987

J oAnn chewed on her fingernails as she flipped through a stack of *American Baby* and *Parents* magazines in the doctor's waiting room. The silent fear of barrenness kept gnawing away at her lifetime dream. Each visit to the doctor seemed to pull out another ribbon of hope from her carefully woven plans. After four years of marriage she was no closer to her home in suburbia, her station wagon, or her seven children.

"JoAnn Taylor, please?" JoAnn pulled her mind back to the present as the nurse led her into a consultation room. "Have a seat, the doctor will be with you shortly."

Dr. Milkamp, the infertility specialist, reviewed JoAnn's medical history, surgeries and tests; then he leaned forward in his chair and folded his hands on his desk. "You're young yet, let's begin with low dosages of weekly hormones first and increase them gradually if necessary. Is your husband willing to be tested?"

"Yes, of course."

Dr. Milkamp explained the possibility of *in vitro*, "There's often a two-year waiting list. With your permission, we'll go ahead and put your name on it." JoAnn nodded her assent. "Understand, of course, there are no guarantees and insurance doesn't pick up the tab." The doctor stood, shook JoAnn's hand, and advised, "Get into an infertility support group. The girl at the desk will give you the name of a contact person."

The doctor was half way out the office door when he turned back toward JoAnn. "One more thing, Mrs. Taylor, how is your marriage?" A puzzled expression crossed JoAnn's face a moment before she answered.

"It's fine." Surprised by the question, she felt she needed to explain further. "I mean, my husband and I have a strong relationship."

"I hope you do. You'll need it." He looked at the floor and scratched the back of his neck. Then he took a deep breath and fixed his gaze past her and proceeded to explain. "It's a long haul. The stress is tremendous. Hormone treatment almost always plays havoc with a woman's emotions, the expenses are staggering, and too often the couple end up blaming each other for their childlessness."

JoAnn didn't give in to the hysteria she felt but she was determined to become a Kool-Aid mom with a jar full of homemade cookies. While the doctor talked, she inhaled deeply, set her chin and stood as tall as her five-feet-three inches allowed. When she was certain he was finished, she tilted her blond head slightly and arched a brow. "Thank you Doctor Milkamp, for being frank with me. When do I see you again?"

T he twelve years of Dr. Ron Herrod's ministry in Louisiana had been rewarding even beyond his expectations. First Baptist Church of Kenner, a suburb of New Orleans, mushroomed under his leadership from an average attendance of 250 in Sunday worship to over 1500.

Then, in spite of the success of his ministry, Ron began to feel unsettled. He wondered if new leadership could take the church on to higher levels of growth. "I don't know if this is from the Lord or not," he confided to Emily.

"Let's pray about it," was her wise counsel.

While they were praying, Ron asked for "a clear word before the end of May."

Shortly after, he received an invitation to preach at the First Baptist Church of Ft. Smith, Arkansas in view of a call as pastor. The date he was to preach? May 31. It seemed a direct answer to their prayers.

He resigned the Kenner church in mid June, and accepted the call to the historic Arkansas church. Following a pastor who had served the congregation for twenty years was a challenge, but Ron never backed away from challenges. He believed the church, well established in Biblical truth, would welcome a strong evangelistic thrust — and the resulting growth. Experienced in such leadership, he planned to assume his new responsibilities July 19.

Ron anticipated the challenge. For Emily, the move meant breaking up the home her children had grown up in, yet she felt good about it. "You know," she told her women's group, "when the Lord moves you somewhere, He always prepares you." Emily's positive attitude radiated peace. "I feel rather up to it."

When asked about the children, Emily answered, "Oh, for Dawn and Joey, since they're in Mobile, Alabama attending college, the family move will affect them little. As for Twila, she's just all excited about new friends and new places. To her it's all a big adventure."

During frequent trips to Arkansas, house hunting, Ron and Emily became close friends with Paul and Kaay Gean, long time, active members of First Baptist, Ft. Smith.

Paul practiced law while Kaay, full time mother to their three daughters, managed their large stone turn-of-the-century home located in the historical section of town. Kaay had a rare gift of hospitality and opened her spacious rooms to exchange students and guest speakers at church on a regular basis.

Always available to help and serve, Kaay escorted Emily from one house to another until the Herrods found an adequate two-level house not far from the church.

The house, sheltered by mature trees and shrubs, stood well below the street level. The driveway angled downhill from the street. The living room opened out onto a back deck that shaded the patio below. The whole back yard was shaded with trees and shrubs except for a sparkling oval pool on the right. A private drive curved onto a quiet street in back which dead-ended at a ravine a short distance to the left.

Because Interstate 540 wound through the ravine, only two houses could be seen from their back yard, one behind and one slightly to the right. There were no neighbors to the left. "The house is okay, and it's close to the church," Emily concluded, "and I really like the seclusion."

Twila, more quiet than usual, perked up with Emily's words. "If we get this house, Mom, can I please choose my own bedroom? Can I have the one at the bottom level? It's much larger and nicer than the one upstairs."

"I don't know why not," Emily responded with a smile. She had been a bit apprehensive about Twila's listlessness during the househunting expedition.

A church member provided the Herrods an apartment where Ron planned to live until they could take possession of their new home. In the meantime, Emily and Twila planned to return to Kenner to finish packing, but Twila became terribly ill.

"According to the tests," Emily explained to Ron after she'd taken Twila to a nearby clinic, "she has mono and the doctor says she's too sick to travel back to Louisiana." Emily ran her fingers through Twila's hair. Being sick made the natural dark around Twila's eyes even darker, accenting her deep-set blue eyes.

As Twila lay curled up on the couch in her father's dark paneled office at their new church, Ron and Emily adjusted their plans. Twila would remain in Ft. Smith with her father while Emily returned to Kenner, finished packing and handled all the details of moving.

During her illness, Twila occasionally spent time with Kaay Gean, but most of the time she stayed at the church with her dad.

Verna Marrow called Eugene for dinner. He came in, neat and clean, and sat down without a word. She studied her son, hesitating a moment before she prayed. Although he didn't object to her praying at the table, she knew it irritated him, but grace had always been a part of her life so she bowed her head and prayed aloud. As soon as she'd finished, Eugene reached for the pizza.

Something about her son had gone wrong even before Clyde and she divorced; now Eugene talked to her only when she asked him a direct question. Even then he'd answer with a grunt or a shrug or a formal, "Yes, ma'am" or "No, ma'am" whenever possible.

She couldn't recall when he began to change toward her but often she tried to remember the times they used to sing church songs together. *"Jesus loves me this I know, for the Bible tells me so. Little ones to Him belong, they are weak but He is strong."* Eugene changed as he got older. Later he stopped going to church and more recently he seemed to live in a world of his own.

Verna wondered what had happened to her sensitive little boy. She could still remember how confused and hurt he'd be and how he'd cry after his dad had treated him so cruelly. She'd felt so helpless watching, yet had not dared to interfere. It was the same kind of helpless feeling she had now as she looked at him across the table.

Eugene wasn't as tall as his Uncle George but he had his jaw line and dark hair. Verna had said so a couple of times but learned not to mention George around Eugene. For some reason he hadn't seemed to get over his uncle's death. Eugene would get a strange, almost frightening look in his eyes and storm out of the house at the mention of George's name and then she was never sure how late it would be before her son would return.

Verna regretted the unnatural silence at the table and found it hard eating her meals with her son who had become a stranger.

It had happened after his dad left. She remembered how often she'd blamed Eugene. Even now at times she blamed him. She couldn't help the way she felt; the things she'd said. Still, it was too late when she realized she had already lost him.

He was a stranger to her now, a distant, sullen stranger who drank. She remembered how she'd cried the first time the police brought him home drunk. Since then she'd gotten angry, violent actually, but she couldn't help herself and she always apologized. Every time, she was sure she apologized.

The only words they exchanged were "Please pass," and "Thank you." *At least he was clean and polite. I have that to be thankful for*, Verna thought. The phone rang and broke the strained silence. Verna answered it.

"It's Betty." Verna passed the phone across the table to Eugene. She'd always liked her friendly neighbor.

"Yes, ma'am."

"Oh, Eugene, I'm glad I caught you. I knew you'd be over any day to mow the yard, it's been growing so fast this spring. Anyway, I wanted to tell you I'm going to be gone and for you to just come on in. You know where the key is. And do you mind carrying some boxes upstairs for me? I've been sorting some things down in the laundry room. You can't miss them. If you can get them up to the front door I can call Goodwill or somebody to come get them. Okay?" Betty seldom waited for an answer. "I'll put a check on the kitchen counter and there's soda in the fridge if you want it. Stay out of the beer though, you're too young to be drinking."

"Yes, ma'am." Eugene was usually available to do chores for his next door neighbor who lived alone since her own kids were grown and off to college.

She knew Eugene drank; that he'd had a couple of speeding tickets. "Nothing so bad about a drink now and then, Eugene," she said in her friendly, motherly fashion, "But to start getting tickets the year you get your driver's license ... "

Eugene knew she'd paused to draw on her cigarette so he didn't say anything. "My husband was a good man until he got to drinking. I didn't want him ruining the kids. Besides, I couldn't take it anymore. Now don't I sound bossy, I didn't mean to start harping. See ya later, Eugene."

"Yes, ma'am," he said again before he handed the phone back to his mother.

Eugene looked at his mother as she put the phone back in its cradle. He felt only disgust for her, even more for her than the father she'd chosen for him. Lately he'd even entertained the thought that she was the cause of his dad's drinking; of their divorce. She could be so nice, talk so religious whenever she needed to. For a moment, their eyes met.

"I wish you'd go to church with me Sunday. You used to go all the time, you know."

"What good does it do?" Eugene got up from the table. "I used to pray, too, until I decided I didn't need another 'father'." Verna opened her mouth to say something but Eugene stalked out of the room. For a reason he didn't try to understand, he realized it felt good to make his mother hurt.

It took an hour for Eugene to mow Betty's yard, then in the solitude of her house he finished his second beer before going down to the laundry room. He had no problem finding the boxes and carrying them upstairs.

Not wanting to return home, he wandered through the house and enjoyed the solitude. He liked the feeling of dominance that swept over him as he invaded the privacy of the master bedroom and the master bath. Eugene saw the nylons on the towel rod. He fingered them, let them slide through his fingers before twisting them into a knot and dropping them to the floor.

Again in the master bedroom he noticed a beige slip over the back of the chair, with another pair of nylons. They felt smooth and cool against the back of his hand. He caught Betty's fragrance from them before he draped them on the chair again in a manner which satisfied him.

Gradually an overwhelming dark need overpowered his thoughts. Suddenly driven, Eugene began pulling open drawers until he found the lacy undergarments. He reached to the bottom of the stack, and slipped a bit of lacy softness into his pocket. Later, under the cover of darkness, he took a walk and satisfied his secret addiction.

Ahhhhhh! It is so eeeeeasy to mold some wills into mine. These puny humans from so-called "dysfunctional" families. They have no concept of "right" or "normal" by the Creator's standards. It is so eeeeeasy to sow my thoughts into Eugene's family; to slip them counterfeit solutions.

Barring the piteous effects of some overzealous prayer warrior or the remote possibility that Eugene would recognize and desire God's love, I'll have the whole family destroyed — forever.

Mornin', Twila, how are you feeling today?" Janey
Spencer, Dr. Herrod's secretary, took an immediate
liking to Twila. "That dad of yours. I can tell already, he's
somethin' else." Janey's laughter filled the office.

"Has he gotten upset and preached you one of his sermons
yet? We've got the ones he uses at home all numbered."
Janey chuckled at Twila's frankness. "Mostly he's short on
patience, so we hear his sermon on time management often."

"Now, Twila, you don't need to be worrying about your
daddy. I assure you he's a real good boss and has been quite
patient with all of us." Janey folded a letter she'd just taken
from the typewriter and was putting it in an envelope. "But
I did tell my husband last night, I said, 'Ben, I think I've been
in training for the last nineteen years, just getting ready for
the new preacher.'"

"Yeah, he's a good dad, too. But Ms. Janey, if you ever get
on his bad side, or if he gets really upset about something,
all you have to do is go get him a chocolate malt." Janey burst
into a peal of laughter.

"Thank you, Twila," she said. "I'll just remember that."

Emily joined Ron and Twila in time to take part in the
Sunday School Frontier Round Up Day in August and to
register Twila as a freshman in Chaffin Junior High School.

Carolyn Plummer felt called to teaching the ninth grade
girls' Sunday School class at First Baptist as certainly as any
preacher felt called to a pulpit. Beautiful, petite, with her
short black hair turned under, Mrs. Plummer was the model

of femininity. Her love for her class extended beyond the Sunday morning hour and all her girls knew it. She welcomed her new fall class the same way she opened all her classes, with homemade brownies and a share time. "As long as you sit like the young ladies you are, you may sit where you're most comfortable," she always said when visitors came. Sometimes the girls sat on chairs, other times they sat on the floor.

"Tell me what's happened in your lives this week," she'd say. Then she'd listen to them talk, tuning into their moods, their concerns and stresses of the past week.

From time to time, one girl or another would say, "Ms. P, I just can't get along with Mom." Twila, was as open as the others in her class and admitted, "Ms. P, it seems that no matter what I do, I'm just not going to be able to get along with Mom at times."

"What you have to understand, girls, is that although you're family, you are still two different individuals and right now you're in the process of developing your own individual personalities."

"Take Twila, for example," said Amy Nunly as she made exaggerated motions. "I've learned that she's a very organized individual and likes to do everything in a certain way. You should see how she arranges her Teddy bears on the floor when she takes her bedspread off her bed at night."

The class burst into knowing giggles. Most of them had eaten hamburgers with Twila and knew she had to assemble hers "just so."

"Your mother is also a very organized and orderly person and chances are you end up clashing." Carolyn took over the conversation again. "There are two good reasons for this and neither of them need to make you feel guilty. First off, women are competitive and since you're all becoming women, your natural competitive spirit is showing up.

"The other reason is that although you both have similar traits you have your own individual thought processes and methods. Usually conflict arises when we resent having to do something someone else's way."

"But why do I have to always do it Mom's way?" A spontaneous chorus of "yeahs" followed Twila's question.

"Let me tell you just what it's like being a mother, the way I see my Alice and Brian. Brian's a young man now and Alice is a year younger than you all. I brought them home as cuddly helpless newborns and I've given my life to training them. It's the responsibility God has given me as their mother. Although I want them to grow up and be responsible adults I dread the day when they won't need me anymore."

"Gee, I never thought of it from my mother's viewpoint." Again, Twila voiced the thoughts of the other girls in her class.

Although the Ft. Smith area boasted over 100,000 in population, most residents were native to Arkansas and often when newcomers arrived from large cosmopolitan cities they felt they had moved back in time. The status quo is revered and anything or anyone different became the subject of talk.

Twila and Emily suffered most from culture shock. Twila had attended the Christian School at the First Baptist Church of Kenner. Kent Lumbard, the principal, called her "the orange juice of the day." Twila saw people as individuals to enjoy and never noticed skin color or the clothes a person wore. She loved everyone equally and assumed they loved her. Now, in a public school she discovered most people chose their friends by different standards. "You won't believe what happened in school today, Mom." Twila had just walked through the door and the pitch of her voice revealed her level of anger.

"No, Sweetheart, I probably won't." Emily had just emptied a small package of blackeyed peas into a large soup kettle. She could tell her daughter was more than a little upset. "What happened?"

"Two girls actually came up to me in the hall and pulled the neck of my shirt back so they could see what label I was wearing." Twila dumped her books on the round kitchen table and stormed to the refrigerator. "Around here, if you don't wear the right clothes, or live in the right part of town you're an outcast. It's stupid!" Twila took a slice of cheese from the refrigerator and began tearing off small bites. "What's worse, they're racist. Mother, if I dared to ask a black friend to spend the night with me, we'd never hear the end of it."

Twila continued to vent her frustration as she opened first one cupboard door and then another. "It's as if there is an unwritten code that dictates who you associate with, who you talk to." Twila filled a glass with ice and opened a can of soda.

"It's a caste system, and the kids whose parents have lived here all their lives and have respected family names and money are at the top of the social ladder. From there on down, it's your blood lines, skin color, where you live, what you wear and what kind of car your parents drive. It's dumb!" The Coke hissed as she poured it; she waited for the foam to settle and abruptly changed the subject.

"Mom, we haven't gotten a Happy Meal for a long time."

"Sure haven't. I wonder what the toy is this week." Emily had started her own collection, much to the chagrin of the whole family. "I know you think I'm silly, but one of these days when you bring home grandbabies, you'll see how smart I am."

The tension within the church did not wane with the summer heat. Dr. Herrod was stymied. Throughout his previous twenty-nine years of pastoring, he'd confidently concluded that given time, prayer and perseverance he could resolve any problem or situation that might present itself within a church. Yet in Ft. Smith, nearly every idea, every plan he proposed seemed to end in deadlock. He'd never been so perplexed.

To make matters worse he could do little to protect Emily and Twila from the atmosphere in the church and community. He knew Emily felt more stress than she'd ever known in their ministry. "The one thing I could never endure, Em," he'd said on more than one occasion, "would be to see you or our children suffer unjustly."

JoAnn appreciated John's pragmatic approach to life. She liked to hear him talk. They spent hours talking, openly sharing their feelings and praying together. The hormone shots had accomplished little more then the expected roller coaster of emotional upheaval. Since seeing the infertility specialist they'd had even more to discuss. More decisions to make.

In vitro, they learned, involved surgically implanting as many as eight of their own fertilized eggs. "That means if all eight were successfully implanted at least six would have to be aborted," JoAnn explained to John.

"And, I assume, implanting two greatly reduces the chance of success?"

"Exactly."

They agreed the second choice was the only one they could live with. For encouragement they turned to a support group; just being with others experiencing the same frustrations helped. Still, in other ways it created more stress. They learned that the Commonwealth of Massachusetts had an all inclusive health plan. "It even pays for *in vitro*," one young lady explained.

"Lot of good that will do us here in Missouri, huh," JoAnn commented. She'd already grown accustomed to writing out $1,600 checks on a fairly regular basis for medical expenses.

"You know of course," one hopeful father explained to John, "That most places accept major credit cards."

"That's what we understand," John commented. "I wonder, though, if there wouldn't be an interest rate advantage with some other lending institution?"

"Well, we've got it all figured out. Now we're not making this public outside this group, but we're using our credit cards, pay only the interest on them, and once we get a baby we'll file Chapter 11. There's no way I can pay off all that debt."

"I don't agree with what some of them are planning to do," JoAnn said later as she and John talked together, "but I can understand their feelings."

JoAnn and her new friends never considered the possibility of *in vitro* not working.

D avid Gibson won Twila's heart when he came to Ft. Smith's First Baptist Church to provide music for the mission conference. "He's cool, Dad, the way he related to the kids and he's got a great sense of humor. Everyone liked the way he led the Bible studies. I think he'd be a great youth minister. He lives in Van Buren, so he wouldn't even have to move."

"There's no doubt he'd be great for the position but David's a pretty gifted musician, Twila, and may not want to narrow his ministry primarily to youth."

"Well, it wouldn't hurt to ask, would it?"

After prayer and consideration, Ron contacted David Gibson. David accepted the call to join the First Baptist church staff as youth minister starting the first Sunday in January.

About this time Dawn and Joey moved to Arkansas. Joey to attend the University of Arkansas in Fayetteville and Dawn to live at home and work. Soon after the New Year, David, Dawn and Joey became acquainted.

E very week Dr. Milkamp increased JoAnn's hormone injections. Even though she experienced the expected mood swings, she never let on at work. No one knew she couldn't conceive; no one knew her heartache. She even kept her composure when other employees asked for a personal day off to have an abortion. It seemed so unfair.

Shopping sprees provided JoAnn emotional release and when her infertility expenses didn't require her total paycheck, she'd come home with something to boost her morale. One day she had two matching, formal living-room chairs delivered and in place in their living room when John came home. "I had some money left over," she explained. They had a mutual agreement not to go into debt.

Work for JoAnn picked up as the holidays drew close. So did her longing for a child. Her emotions were more unpredictable than ever. The sight of Santa Claus with children on his knee triggered tears one noon hour as she wandered through nearby Chesterfield Mall. Yet, before the day had ended, she was disturbed by something even more unnerving.

"John," she shared as soon as they had both arrived home from work. "I just found out this afternoon that one of the girls who recently had an abortion did it because she was pregnant from rape. She didn't believe in abortion but she figured no one would want a child that was conceived by rape. Could you love a child that was a product of rape?"

John studied his wife's questioning gaze. "I see such a child as a victim as much as the mother. I can't think of anytime God's love excluded children of rape. Yes, JoAnn, I believe I could love a child of rape."

40

1988

M orning, Ashley." Carolyn Plummer smiled warmly as she greeted her girls as they arrived at Sunday school. "Liz, you look so pretty today. Corrin, help yourselves to the brownies and pass them around."

"Oh, Ms. P," Twila moaned as she breezed into the classroom. "I thought I'd never get here in time. The clothes I set out last night just didn't fit the weather today, and I couldn't figure out what to wear, and Dad was in a hurry and Mom's always late. It's been a terrible week." Twila plopped herself down. "Hi Amy, did you get the chair you wanted in band?"

Carolyn let the girls chatter briefly. Then she asked, "Twila, what's been so terrible this week?" Tension punctuated the sudden silence in the room as the girls looked from one to another.

"Ms. P," Twila answered, suddenly serious, "A girl at school got pregnant. Everybody's talking about it."

Amy Nunley, Twila's closest friend, shared her feelings. "Ms. P, the thing that really bothers me is she seems so flippant about it. Like it's no big deal or anything." Several girls nodded agreement with Amy.

"I guess I wonder how I would act if it happened to me." Sarah spoke hesitantly, as though wondering if she dared to be so honest. "I mean, I don't plan for it to ever happen but then I don't suppose any girl ever does."

"I heard her parents are rich enough, so they're sending her to live in Dallas at some home for unwed mothers," Coralea added.

"That would be awful." Corrin, more quiet by nature, put her hand over her mouth. She couldn't imagine leaving the close security of her home.

"Yeah, but it'd be worse living here, everybody talking about you, asking questions and all." No one argued with Twila's conclusion and Mrs. Plummer took over the conversation.

"To me, my virginity was a very precious gift which I kept for my husband and no one else. On my wedding day, I knew that I was the first person for him and he was the first person for me. Girls, experience isn't necessary. When you do get married, you'll understand how wonderful it is to learn together how to express your love."

The class sat silently, taking in each carefully spoken guideline Ms. Plummer gave them. "You're at the age when you need to decide what kind of bride you want to be and determine not to let yourself get into situations where temptation is possible. You don't want to go into marriage with scars and guilt and have flashbacks of times that were wrong and painful to remember.

"Protect your virginity, because once you've given it away, you'll never get it back. It's gone."

Virginity! Aaah! Yes, little girls, your virtue is sooooo important. This Sunday school teacher's moralizing is soooo futile. Warn them! Go ahead. I control more and more of the real influences in their lives. Movies, TV, magazines. My message is sooooo much more glamorous than yours! Can you make stars in their eyes? Can you flash lurid thoughts in their minds? Can you even protect them from the mixed instructions they receive from their schools?

How do you think you can counteract me, Mssssssss. Plummer? But you have given me an idea. The temptations I put before your pastor are ineffective, but his daughter? Ahhhh, he would be devastated if she were put in jeopardy. I could destroy the testimony of the whole family with one blow.

Twila! Their sweeeet little girl who is blossoming into womanhood. Yesssss, the child they love soooo much. I shall destroy their faith by robbing her of her innocence.

But how?

Intellectually, Eugene thrived on the disciplined, predictable atmosphere of the classroom. His teachers perceived his aloofness as mature independence from peer pressure, not insecurity. His high grades they considered marks of a super achiever, not of a child starving for acceptance. Few, if any, recognized the crippled, hurting boy inside the handsome, growing young man.

Emotionally, Eugene's health continued to deteriorate. School and studies and the cheers on the football field couldn't dim his troubled memories, and drinking numbed his craving for love and acceptance but never filled the aching void.

Over lunch he watched the kids around him. *God. How can they find so much to talk about? And the way they touch each other. I would never let a girl touch me. Of course, why would she want to? No girl would ever consent to date me. I won't give them a chance to say no. Did I say God? That's wrong. Not if He doesn't exist. Why do I exist?* Eugene felt safer eating alone.

The class bell rang. His days were routine; so were his nights.

Most nights, Eugene roamed the streets. It was a way to avoid his mother. If she wasn't nagging, she was sullen, quiet and watchful. He could feel her eyes studying him. She brooded.

Eugene mostly roamed the street behind his house. Until recently he'd wander to the end of it, sit on the slope and watch the cars on Highway 540 below rush by. Since the day alone in Betty's bedroom he'd added another interest to his solitary life. The lighted window in the lower level of the house behind his.

Eugene lost himself in the dark shadows of the dense foliage and stealthily made his way to the retaining wall only a few feet from what he'd learned was a girl's bedroom. Several times a week he'd settle himself into the dark vault formed by the wall and the bushes.

From the seclusion of his cave he listened to her music and her singing. *I wonder who she's writing to? Must have a lot of friends. She sure has a big collection of Teddy bears. Her own phone. Lucky — who would I call if I had one? I wonder if it is a boy or girl she's talking to? I never knew girls did their nails so often. That must be her mother. They smiled the whole time they talked. I can't remember the last time Mom kissed me.*

The lights flicked out. Eugene pulled from his pocket the soft, small garment he'd taken from Betty's dresser drawer and assuaged his feelings of helpless.

J oAnn Taylor readily acknowledged she'd been raised in a privileged lifestyle. Her parents not only had money, they had a good relationship with their four children and raised them in a happy home. Now, married to a man she both loved and respected, JoAnn for the first time in her life found herself facing a situation she couldn't fix. Infertility was the first major test of her faith.

"Medically, there's nothing more we can do," Dr. Milkamp explained. "Your tests have shown that you both test in the lower range of fertile. In all probability, if either of you had a different spouse with a higher level of fertility, you could each parent a child."

Both John and JoAnn grappled with feelings of worthlessness caused from their inability to create life. Each

felt the urge to blame the other but chose instead to take
shelter in their unconditional love.

Once past the initial disappointment, JoAnn shared a
new insight. "I've come to realize I don't have to experience
birth, I only need to have a child. I've taken care of so many
different children, I know I could love any child."

"If those are your true feelings, JoAnn, it seems like
adoption is our only other option."

That evening, they began praying for the baby the Lord
was going to give them.

It took several evenings before they settled on a small,
independent adoption facility, Hope Agency. "Listen John."
They were sitting on the couch in their living room,
surrounded with agency packets as JoAnn read aloud, 'In
order to make our services most available, we not only
network with other adoption agencies, we keep constant
contact with crisis pregnancy centers throughout the nation.' "

"Do they have an open or closed policy?"

"Neither. They call their's 'touch adoption.' They say,
'Hope agency encourages a monthly exchange of letters for
the first year, and yearly thereafter. Pictures of the adopted
child may be included if agreeable to both parties. All
correspondence is channeled through the agency in order not
to disclose addresses and to enable Hope Agency to screen
out any revealing information.' "

"It seems that it would be much easier for a mother to
place her child for adoption with that kind of policy." John
reached for the literature and read it for himself. "I like that.
What do you think?"

"I'd love to have a relationship with the mother. Just to
be able to reassure her that her child was loved, and was
okay. Oh, John, I really like that."

Before JoAnn left for lunch the following day she dialed
the number for Hope Agency. She asked a number of specific
questions about the agency and spoke frankly about her
interest in adoption to Ted Watson, the director, before she
requested an application.

"Before we send you a preliminary application, may I ask a few general questions to see if you meet the requirements our clients are looking for?"

"By all means."

"Do you and your husband both profess to be born again Christians? Do you attend church regularly? Do you abstain from the use of alcohol and all illegal drugs? Can you medically substantiate your inability to bear children?"

Satisfied with JoAnn's answers, Ted Watson concluded, "We'll be happy to send you a preliminary application. Keep in mind, application is only to see if you can be considered as potential adoptive parents. It's an initial step only. If you pass it, then we will proceed with detailed analysis of your background and family life. You could be disqualified at any point along the way."

"Thank you," JoAnn replied, almost dizzy with hope. Three weeks after they returned their preliminary application, they received a reply.

Dear Mr. and Mrs. Taylor;

We have received your application for adoption.

If you are selected for further study, you will be notified by mail no later than February 29.

We select applications from a cross-section of society, differing ethnic groups, socio-economic levels and various geographical areas … the children all have various needs. Your parenting skills and other personal qualifications are not our only consideration.

We don't say this to discourage you but to help you be realistic …

JoAnn did feel discouraged and the pamphlet enclosed with the letter didn't help.

The greatest love often experiences the greatest sorrow. We see this everytime a mother places her child for adoption … The number of babies available for adoption has plummeted from 250 a year to 50 enabling us

to place a child with about one of every ten
couples applying.

A professional men's luncheon and weekly Bible study group, "The Truth on Thursday," drew close to 150 persons each week to the Fellowship Hall of First Baptist Church, Ft. Smith. Dr. Herrod generally taught the study but oftentimes the speakers were local professionals. Such was the case with Dr. Larry Hyde, who was a member of the church.

Dr. Hyde was an oversized, self-styled man. He looked as if he'd be at home on some huge earth moving machine, as foreman on a construction site or maybe as a rancher of a big Texas spread. His hair, which he often combed by raking his fingers through it, resembled clean, wind-blown wheat.

When Dr. Hyde stood before the group, he unceremoniously stated, "One of these days I'm going to write a book." He paused and looked around as though he was trying to find his next sentence. "I'm going to title it, 'Every man needs a gynecologist he can trust.' " A ripple of laughter spread through the crowd.

"Some of what I share with you today comes from a part of my life that I refer to as my 'redeemed hall of shame.' I don't have time to tell you some of the horrible things I witnessed during my OB residency. But in retrospect, the most horrible thing to me was not arms and legs and other recognizable parts going by in a clear plastic tube as I terminated a pregnancy. It was, instead, when I found myself insensitive to what I was doing." Dr. Hyde spoke with his head down, slowly pacing the small platform. "My conscience was so seared I had lost the ability to fear God.

"Now, let me give you what in post grad teaching is called a pre-course quiz. What would you do in these four situations?" He turned and started pacing again.

"A young girl is accosted and raped. She conceives an unwanted child and suffers from the memory of the incident. If you were a physician what would you recommend?" He stopped and peered again across the crowd before he continued his narrative.

"A baby is born. It doesn't breath. Time passes." Dr. Hyde was pacing again. "Racing against time you begin resuscitation efforts. More time passes. The child is ventilated and does not respond. Fifteen minutes have passed and you know from years of training there is going to be major brain damage. It's a hopeless situation. Would you allow this child to die?" There was an uncomfortable stir in the audience. The doctor stood still jingling change in his pocket. When the room was silent, he continued.

"You're working in a clinic and receive ultrasound reports showing an unborn child's head and neck have not developed properly and there's a large tumor on the back of its head. There's good reason to believe the child will never be able to function normally. You have the option of deciding whether this pregnancy should continue or not." He turned to his listeners for an answer. "What would you do?"

"My last scenario," he explained, already pacing, "is that of a teenaged girl who hungers for acceptance. She cares for a fellow and the level of intimacy accelerates. She finds herself pregnant and then discovers this man has no real interest in her or his child. She's only eight weeks along, has high school and college ahead and this is going to destroy her life. If you were the girl's parent, how would you counsel her?" Doctor Hyde stood silent for a moment. When he spoke again his voice had lost its professional tone.

"Had I not listened to my wife and to my conscience and the Holy Spirit, I would not have to tell you of my failure... Because of the goodness of God and the grace of God, He has forgiven me." He stepped behind the small podium and gripped its sides.

"I have learned I can't trust my own knowledge. It's incomplete. You see, if you voted to terminate any of these four pregnancies, you would have taken a life of someone who is part of the kingdom of God. The black lady demoralized by rape gave birth to the great soloist, Ethel Waters. The infant who didn't breath for more than fifteen minutes is my oldest daughter, Amy. The girl with the tumor as large as her head is my daughter, Sarah. And the young lady starved for love gave life to my youngest daughter, Kathleen.

"Be very careful when you trust the knowledge of man, the knowledge of science or the intellectual ruling elite, whether they be politicians, teachers or doctors ... "

A puzzled expression wrinkled the corners of JoAnn's eyes as she sat across from John in a booth at Applebee's. "I guess my problem with adoption is not knowing enough about the emotional background or the health of the parents." John reached across the table for JoAnn's hand and cleared his throat.

"Let's look at the problem the other way around," he suggested. "How much of a medical history did you do on me before we agreed to marry? And if I'd had heart disease or diabetes in my history, would you have married me?"

"I don't think I could have resisted you if you'd had three eyes." JoAnn chuckled. "For that matter, how many people today have family histories completely free of such genetic pre-dispositions as cancer, heart disease, or diabetes and how many birth parents even think about such things, much less question them before having their children?"

Later, driving home, JoAnn shared with John, "I listened to a tape of Chuck Swindoll's today and he was talking about adoption being the answer to abortion. What he said made me realize that it's really an honor to adopt. He brought out that couples who adopt model how people become part of God's family. How God reached into humanity and selected an individual and said, 'You're mine.' Let me see if I can quote him. He said, 'The destinies of unwanted children carried to term and adopted bear a distinct mark with eternal dimensions.'"

John smiled a little half smile and nodded his head. "Good insight, I like that."

As they pulled into their driveway, JoAnn shared, "For so long it's seemed as if God has been denying me the very thing I've always wanted most." A tear slid down her cheek.

"Don't you suppose if God is taking away something, it's to make room for something uniquely better for you?"

John cupped his hand under her chin and pecked her on the tip of her nose. JoAnn knew it was his way of saying he understood. The somber mood lifted.

"Come see the headway I've made in the junk room. My biggest problem now is trying to decide how I want to decorate the nursery. Oh, John, isn't that a beautiful word?"

In June pastors and church messengers from across the U.S. met in San Antonio, Texas for the annual meeting of the Southern Baptist Convention. For many, the annual convention is a time to renew acquaintances and catch up on each others' church and family news. Such was the case for Ron and Emily Herrod and the Reverend Miles and Jeanne Seaborn.

For twenty years the Herrods had been friends with the Seaborns. Miles was the pastor at Birchman Baptist in Ft. Worth, Texas. The two couples strolled along the River Walk looking for a Mexican restaurant for a late evening snack.

"So how are things at Birchman?" Ron asked, after they'd given their orders.

"Looks like we'll soon be ready to start construction on our main sanctuary." Miles' round face was radiant. The sanctuary would be the fourth of a five-stage building program for his church membership of nearly three thousand.

"And how was your first year in Ft. Smith?"

"Well now, it's been quite a challenge. We're not making the kind of progress I'd like, but it'll change. It's an old downtown church and some of the membership want to keep the original stone structure for its historical value. Actually, it has become a pigeon roost with severe structural problems. The people are going to have to decide whether to keep their historical monument to the past or prepare for growth and an evangelical thrust into the community."

As the men talked about their churches, their wives talked about their families. Three of the Seaborns' children were married and Jeanne pulled out pictures of grandchildren.

"Well, we're all excited," Emily confided. "Last Christmas the church called a youth minister, David Gibson, and he and Dawn have fallen in love right before our very eyes. Now, they are a picture. He's tall, over six feet and she's shorter than I am." Emily's face glowed with excitement and joy.

"He's been so good for her." He and Joey play off each other and torment poor little Twila half to death. Of course, she just loves it and thinks he'll be the perfect brother-in-law. Ron keeps saying, 'I think we've got a match.' Of course, he'd be thrilled to have another minister in the family. We're sort of thinking something will happen before too long."

Before the summer was over, Dawn was wearing a diamond. Both Ron and David felt their time in Ft. Smith would soon run out, so Dawn made plans for a November wedding.

Mrs. Plummer had mixed emotions on promotion Sunday. She anticipated getting to know the young girls coming into the high school department but she hated to say goodbye to those graduating. After their final lesson together, her eyes filled with tears.

"You all have been so sweet to me at Christmas and on my birthday and you've understood that there are so many of you I can't reciprocate. But I have given you my love. You are my girls. I have kept all of your cards and when I need a pick me up, I get one of them out of my little sunshine box. You have given me so much more than I've given you and you know I will always want to be a part of your lives." Every girl gave a hug and kiss to Mrs. Plummer when they left.

JoAnn? Ted Watson here — from Hope Agency."
"Yes, Mr. Watson?" JoAnn tightened her grip on the telephone.

"Just checking in to see how you and John are doing. We haven't had contact for some time and we wanted to see if you were still interested in adopting."

"We're doing fine, and yes, we're still waiting. Do you have something? I mean, is there a child we're being considered for now?"

"We can never tell those things ahead of time, you know. Mothers can change their minds even after giving birth. We do hope to have something going for you within a few months, however."

"Oh, I hope so."

"Of course, you'll need a car seat because you can't pick up a baby without one."

"Can you be more specific?"

"No, I'm sorry we can't."

"But it would be advisable to get a car seat and basic things?"

"Yes, that would be wise."

The wedding was the most exciting, romantic event Twila could remember. As she proceeded down the aisle in her long gown, she felt honored to be one of her sister's bridesmaids. The rustle of taffeta accompanied the organ as she took her place at the front of the beautiful, old sanctuary. Turning, she watched Dawn, dressed in her gorgeous, white gown and long trailing skirt, floating toward her groom.

As the ceremony progressed Twila couldn't help but dream of her own wedding. *I'm going to wear a white dress for my wedding, too,* she vowed. *I'm going to wait for the special man that God has chosen for me, just like Dawn. No matter what the other girls at school think, I'm going to keep myself pure. I'm going to look into my groom's eyes just like Dawn is doing now. My turn will come. It's worth waiting for.*

December 1988 — March 1989

The prospect of another Christmas without a child dimmed JoAnn's holiday joy. Then, in early December, a letter arrived from the agency. Crazed with anticipation, she ripped the envelope open immediately and read,

```
Dear Friend,
     We are facing a very serious situation and
we are unsure of the impact or outcome. The
request for crisis pregnancy counseling and
maternity care has radically decreased...
```

Due to this dramatic decline for maternity counseling and infants available for adoption, we are temporarily putting a hold on our adoption services...

JoAnn's hopes plummeted even further. "How 'bout let's take a trip after the first of the New Year?" John suggested, hoping to lift his wife's heavy spirit as they trimmed their Christmas tree. "Maybe the Bahamas?"

"Could we?" JoAnn smiled warmly at her husband from the other side of the tree. He always sensed when the discouragement of waiting became too stressful.

Abominable! John and JoAnn are abominable! Their stubborn allegiance to the Creator in spite of their childlessness makes me look like a fool ... but not for long.

I'll utilize a self-righteous well-meaning saint, who is grossly ignorant about infertility, to twist the Truth slightly ... Twisted truths worked so well in the garden.

At the very least I can cause hurt feelings, the breeding ground for bitterness.

W e're studying from Psalm 127 today," Joe Bradley announced to the Sunday School class.

JoAnn cut her eyes briefly toward John — and they exchanged a knowing glance. She flipped the pages of her Bible to the familiar passage. She had read the verses so often, prayed over them, wept over them and at times felt condemned by them. If children were a blessing, and she believed they were, then why was God withholding His blessing from John and her? What had they done wrong? What did they do to deserve the humiliation of seeing the intimacies of their relationship reduced to medical data? She steeled herself and reached over for John's hand, wondering how the passage would be interpreted.

Joe, a young seminary student and father of three small children, began reading, "Behold, children are a gift of the Lord; the fruit of the womb is a reward. Like arrows in the hand of a warrior, so are the children of one's youth. How blessed is the man whose quiver is full of them; they shall not be ashamed." JoAnn relaxed momentarily as Joe spoke about the gift of children.

"The most common definition of a quiverfull is five," Joe stated. "It disturbs me that so many couples today are not having children because of careers or they are postponing their families until they are financially comfortable."

"What about people who can't have children?" JoAnn asked.

"Well, they need to continue praying and really examine their lives." Joe looked directly at JoAnn as he talked. "Maybe it's because she's working and that stress of working is preventing her from conceiving."

JoAnn felt as if she'd been slapped across the face.

It was a silent ride from church to Union Station, a favorite spot for lunch. Holding hands, they meandered past the line of food shops before they settled on Greek spinach pies and salads from Athens Eatery.

Over the small, round table for two, JoAnn began to vent her frustrations. " 'Pray more,' Joe says. How much is 'more?' Do the Joe's of Christendom have enough wisdom to know that? And what about examining myself; are children mere brownie points God hands out when we've prayed enough or reached some particular degree of perfection?"

"He made me feel a little defensive, too."

Two weeks later a fat letter from Hope Agency arrived in the mail. "We've been selected for further study!" Overjoyed, JoAnn shook the letter in John's face. "Honey, do you realize we're one day closer? We've got a toe in the door."

For the next two months the Taylors worked to complete all the detailed application papers. Pictures of themselves and their home, floor plans, savings accounts, household budget and character references all had to be provided, but the hardest part was writing their individual biographies.

The Taylors prayed for the birth mother and JoAnn read all she could find on adoption. "John, one thing in particular is necessary for women of unplanned pregnancies. That is for them to do everything necessary to make the pregnancy a positive experience. Their mental attitude does affect the child."

"Then let's pray that whatever the circumstances, the birth mother will have a healthy attitude and positive experience," John replied, "and let's trust the Lord to make that possible."

At first it amused Eugene to watch the girl take one outfit after another out of her closet, as if she were shopping, finally deciding on one and putting it across a chair, then setting out her shoes, earrings and the like. Her whole routine intrigued him — the nightly letter writing, the fingernails, the phone calls, music always playing. But it was her contentment — her happiness — that needled him most. *Would you be so happy if you had my dad?* he thought. *What makes you think those people you write to and those people you call even want to hear from you? What makes you think you're so special? Haven't I seen you at school? Swim team. Yeah. You're not even that great. You're all fluff. Dumb blonde. Mom's a blonde. I hate blondes.*

Eugene had watched the house from different corners of the back yard. *Mother doesn't work. Dad is in the study at the other end of the house from the bedroom window and studies a couple of nights a week. Dog can be real noisy.*

Eugene discovered there were always a couple of hours on Wednesday nights and Sunday nights when no one was home. Curiosity prompted him to see if the sliding patio door was locked. He checked it several times. It wasn't. It glided quietly on its track, he noticed, and made only a slight click when the latch caught.

R on, can you get the phone?" Emily called from the flower bed in the back yard. For years she screened the phone calls at home so Ron wouldn't be disturbed during his morning study time.

He waved his answer from the screen door and headed for his office with a fresh cup of coffee.

"Who called?" she asked when she came in later in her stocking feet, holding her muddy, grass-stained tennis shoes.

"Security system salesman."

"My goodness." Emily turned and headed for the laundry room, talking as she went. "I believe that's the third time since we moved here that someone has tried to sell us a system." They had had a security system installed in their home in Kenner and discussed whether or not to install one in their new home. "Ron, do you think it's necessary?"

"Hardly. Ft. Smith's a much smaller town and doesn't begin to have the same crime rate. Besides, we live in a quiet, established neighborhood."

JoAnn's hands shook as she opened the envelope and scanned the letter. "John, we've been accepted in the New York infertility clinic! Did you hear me John? The clinic says we have an eight percent chance."

Before John could even answer, JoAnn ran to the phone and started dialing her friend, Donna Mills, in Texas. As soon as Donna answered, JoAnn blurted out enthusiastically, "The clinic in New York says we have an eight percent chance! Donna, isn't it wonderful?"

"Where will you stay?"

"A hotel near the clinic."

"Do they say what the medical expenses will run?"

"Yeah, $12,000."

"JoAnn, listen to me." There was a long pause before Donna continued. "You're not reading that objectively. What have you spent already? How many thousands of dollars? And they're offering to let you spend $12,000 for two weeks, plus your hotel, plus your food and you're guaranteed a ninety-two percent chance of failure?"

"But Donna, it's an eight percent chance."

"I hear you, JoAnn, but do you see the failure rate? They're playing mind games. They know how badly you want a baby and they're offering a chance. I guess what I'm trying to ask is, can you live with spending that much more money and still not having a baby? Have you two decided where the stopping point is? Haven't you done all that's reasonably possible to do?" Donna waited and heard only a long silence.

"John's got the barbecue ready." JoAnn's voice was flat. "I've got to go." As she put the receiver down the hard reality of Donna's loving words hit home.

Spring 1989

E mily was the last to sit down at the Easter Sunday dinner of roast beef, gravy and rice and banana pudding. She looked to her husband as a signal that all was ready.

"Joey, it's good to have you home again. Would you ask the blessing for us?"

"Sure, Dad," he replied, reaching for Twila's hand on one side and David's on the other.

Meal time for the Herrods was as much a time for fun as food. After discussing Emily's good cooking, the Sunday morning attendance and baseball, Joey switched to Twila's love life.

"Let's see, Twila, you're fifteen now..."

"Almost sixteen," she reminded Joey.

"Almost sixteen, eh? That's even more dangerous. What unsuspecting sucker do you have on your line?"

"None. I've only double dated a couple of times."

"Same fellow?"

"Yes, but..."

"She's having a hard time getting to know him," David said, joining in Joey's sport.

"Twila, my outgoing, talkative, friendly and uninhibited sister, is having trouble getting to know a boy?" Joey exaggerated each word with mock surprise.

"Now, David, that's not true," Twila defended. "Steve James is really nice."

"How do you know, Goofball? He never says anything." David grinned and glanced at Joey. "I've noticed she always picks the silent type."

"Has to." Joey took a drink of water. "Gives her more opportunity to talk."

"Now wait a minute. That's not fair. Steve talks and he's really a sweet, sensitive guy." Twila tried hard to be serious but her eyes twinkled and her voice invited challenge. "He's just quiet around strangers, that's all and I don't do all the talking."

"Now easy, Twila." Joey held his hand up in a peaceful gesture. "We all love you. It's simply a commonly known fact that women who do all the talking are happiest marrying men who don't talk. Who knows, this Steve may end up being a permanent fixture in your life."

"He's not a fixture," Twila defended. Then in a subdued voice she added, "He's been going steady for the last two weeks with another girl from school."

JoAnn? Ted Watson here, from Hope Agency."

"Yes, Mr. Watson?" She was in her office at work and stretched the phone cord taut to nudge her door closed. No one at work knew she was trying to adopt; she couldn't face the questions. Now, hearing Ted's name made her heart race.

"I needed to verify a couple of dates with you..."

JoAnn swallowed hard and provided the information in question before she dared to ask if they had a child in mind.

"It's probably too soon yet but in God's time, you'll have a baby. We hope within a few months to have something going for you."

"I sure hope so." JoAnn hung up with a sense of hope and urgency she hadn't felt in months. It was time she decided how to furnish the nursery.

I'm home." Twila didn't wait for an answer before she bounced down the stairs to her room and dumped her books and clothes bag on her bed. She changed quickly from her swimsuit and damp clothes into her mis-matched PJs before ducking into the bathroom to wash the chlorine from her face. Her hair she'd wash in the morning.

Twila made a beeline to the kitchen as soon as she'd dried her face and hung her wet things in the laundry room. "What's for supper? I'm starved."

"You can order a pizza. It's the ladies' spring banquet at the church tonight, remember? I've got to be there, Twee Dee, and Daddy's supposed to speak, so you're on your own tonight. How was practice?"

"Okay I guess. I shouldn't have taken competitive swimming though. I'd have fit in the recreational class better."

"Is it really that hard?"

"It is if you can't do the butterfly. I can handle the backstroke all right, sorta —." Twila went to the phone, checked the list of numbers taped to the side of it and started dialing. "I mean, I'm not as good as a lot of them but I'm better than some. Hi, I'd like to order a medium pepperoni with cheese."

Twila watched TV and studied from the middle of her parents' king-sized bed until 9:00 p.m. Leaving the kitchen light on, she headed down to her room to begin her nightly debate over which outfit to wear to school the next day. Finally, she spread her clothes across a chair, and deliberated over accessories. This early childhood game had become a refined, daily habit.

T ension was building at Eugene Marrow's home. "I still can't believe you were so stupid. First you drive your father out and then you quit school!" Verna had berated Eugene continuously since he had dropped out of school shortly after Christmas. "At least he put food on the table. You can't even do that, you dummy. You had less than a semester left and you'd have had a scholarship."

Eugene withdrew even more into himself as a defense against his mother's escalating and caustic aggression. Her unpredictable rages became a knife, cutting, and gradually severing what remained of nature's maternal bond.

"Eugene, how do you expect to make it in life? You're drinking more all the time. You stay out half the night whenever you take a notion. Do you expect me to support you all your life? It's time to become a man and take some responsibility in life."

Verna winced under Eugene's look of sullen disdain. "Why do you look at me like that? Why?" A cynical smile cut across his face. "What have I done to make you hate me so much?" The tone of Verna's brittle voice suddenly changed.

"You know, it would really help if you'd get back in church," she purred. "Won't you please come to church with me?" Eugene stalked wordlessly out of the house.

Her words ignited his buried anger like a lit match would a dynamite fuse and with every thought the fuse burned closer to the devastating power compressed inside him. He hated her for not believing in him. The thought made his hands cold and his body shiver even in the hot humid summer night.

He hated her for not protecting him from his Uncle George — for praising her brother and not knowing the real truth about him. He hated her for not protecting him all those times when his dad was drunk and mean and teasing. He hated her for not defending him when his dad said he wasn't a man, that he was a wimp. Loneliness knotted his stomach.

Eugene's breath was fast and shallow; the muscles in his jaws stood out hard, working. He clenched his fists. He felt as if something in him would explode when he recalled her words. *It's time you become a man.*

But I am a man! Eugene screamed to himself. He knew he was intelligent. He'd made the honor roll, he was physically strong, he'd been on first string. Yet, neither achievement nor the protective wall of solitude he'd wrapped around himself ever completely sheltered him from the pain of rejection. Eugene felt deserted by his father.

Verna's nagging increased. "Why are you always by yourself? Where do you go every night? Why don't you date? You should be in church."

Verna had been hounding him all through supper. Finally she cried, "Oh, God, how I prayed you'd grow up to be a man like your Uncle George, but instead you've driven your father away. Get out of my house! Get out of my sight!"

Eugene fled through the back door. Pity he had felt for his mother not knowing the truth about George had turned to contempt. Anger at having to take the brunt of his parents' failed marriage had chilled to bitterness. He had no place to go. He felt abandoned.

The events of the evening had woven into place that predictable yet inexplicable twist in Eugene's mind which transformed him. No longer was he the depressed and insecure victim he had been in his childhood. The boy who was always striving for approval. He had become a calculating aggressor. The ancient "eye for an eye" had become his life and he had some catching up to do.

Standing alone in the darkness outside a lighted window no longer satisfied the growing need he felt, neither did his other dark and solitary pastimes. For days now he had felt the need to lash out. To get even.

Eugene wandered aimlessly to the end of his street. The spring air was heavy. Exhaust fumes from the highway mingled with the smell of damp, moldy earth. He kicked hard, scattering a clod of dirt, then swore at the dirt that clung to the toe of his shoe.

Voices drew his attention, a car door slammed, then another. The neighbors' Cadillac drove away. Partially hidden by the spring foliage, Eugene leaned his shoulder against a tree.

Only two in the car. The girl's home alone.

He waited, an idea forming in his mind. A pizza delivery car drove up. *Dinner delivered. She's probably alone for the evening.* Eugene looked at his watch. *Dark in another hour and a half, plenty of time to think this through.* He squatted down and sat at the base of the tree.

For an hour he pulled grass, one blade at a time. He'd bite the ends, split the shafts with his fingernail then tie the slender threads in knots. By the time it was too dark to see, his plan was complete. Keeping to the familiar shadows, Eugene moved closer to the house. He liked the feel of stalking his prey. Then he waited for total darkness.

In a short time the light in the upstairs window flicked off. That was his cue. As he stood to his feet he felt one large jolt in his chest — his heart had skipped a beat. His mouth became a desert.

Eugene entered the unlocked door easily enough. The patio was well shaded by the deck above. Once inside, he stood silently in the dark shadows of the large, open, wood-paneled family room. He'd seen her snap her bedroom light on.

From all the times he'd watched outside the windows, Eugene was familiar with the rooms on the lower level of the house. An open stairway and wall divided the basement lengthwise. The stairway stopped at the door of the girl's bedroom to the right. To the left was another bedroom with a bath between. To his right, a door slightly ajar, led to the pastor's office. To Eugene's left, a large screen TV and fireplace lined the wall.

He stood diagonally across from the only lighted room. Her door stood ajar and he watched her familiar routine. He listened to her music. This time it was something religious and she sang along with it.

Eugene didn't analyze her happiness, nor did he name his envy. For days he'd nursed a growing sense of inadequacy and need to retaliate. His planned revenge. His dad would know Eugene's disgrace. His mom would feel his helpless abandonment.

Humiliating memories crowded Eugene's thinking. He remembered his father pinching him and laughing when he cried. He felt the old familiar sense of helplessness, the same loss of control he had when his dad wouldn't stop tickling him. He clenched his fists. A wave of heat surged through his body. He felt the sticky sweat of his armpits. His mouth was too dry to swallow.

The girl was out of sight when Eugene heard talking. *The phone. Of course, she talks a lot, must have a lot of friends.* He heard her laughter, soft and — *what does it remind me of?* Suddenly Eugene remembered another laugh — his Uncle George's laugh. Eugene's mind crowded with memories. Memories that brought familiar urges. Swelling urges demanding gratification. Gratification that no longer satisfied, no longer soothed his shattered ego, no longer pacified his seething rage.

Eugene could hear water running in the bathroom. He'd wait until she finished brushing her teeth and went back into her bedroom before he moved. Confident with the anticipation of vengeance, he moved with ease, his steps silent on the carpeted floor. The defenselessness of the little female beckoned him. He could easily overpower her. Power. Surging power. *I feel so good.* Eugene smiled, knowing he'd found a way to prove himself. She was only an object to conquer. A way to get even. A way to destroy.

Twila, suddenly alert, turned from her closet. She saw the stranger standing silently in her doorway, casually leaning against the door frame. She noted his navy blue slacks, blue plaid shirt and well groomed dark hair before she saw the arrogant smile creep slowly across his face. Her surprise turned to shock, then horror, as she comprehended his intent. She turned her face from his hideous smirk and backed away.

Deliberately, Eugene stepped toward her. *Maybe I can get around him ... let him take another step.* Quickly, she side-stepped, twisting to get away.

His hand gripped her arm like an iron jaw biting into her flesh. She refused to look at him. Expecting to be strong from swimming she pulled hard, trying to wrench her arm from his grasp. Her strength was nothing against his.

Eugene whipped his free hand hard across her chest, knocking her down across the bed. Seeing her helplessness, her terror, he felt imbued with power. He didn't even have to say a word.

Twila averted her head, refusing to see his sickening smile. They struggled. Pinned beneath his rigid strength she sensed her futile efforts. Faint shafts of reason pierced through her black hysteria. It was then she realized self-preservation demanded surrender.

Twila closed her eyes and her mind to the reality she endured. *I won't think about it ... it will be over soon ... it will be over ... it will be soon ... over soon ... over.*

Twila lay exposed and humiliated, daring not to move until the faint click of the patio storm door closing signaled she was alone. Pulling her clothes together she ran and locked the door behind the intruder. Blinded by tears she stumbled back to her bed again. There she sat, stunned, rigid, silently crying. Gradually the numbness left her. Reality closed in.

She wiped at her tears and felt again the stranger's breath on her face. She felt dirty. Filthy. Contaminated. She stared at the clock, willing herself to comprehend the time while forcing herself not to see the haughty smirk that still leered at her from the corners of her mind.

It was late. Her parents would be home any time. She had to be in bed so they wouldn't ask questions. Twila's legs shook as she stood at the sink scrubbing her face, her neck, her arms, her mouth. She longed for a shower to wash away the eternity she'd just endured but she didn't have time.

She forced herself back into her room — back to her bed. She felt a sticky wetness between her legs. *Blood! Clean clothes. I've got to put on clean clothes.* Frantically she pulled clean clothes from her drawer and changed. She swallowed the bitterness that rose in her throat as she stooped to bury the evidence of her bleeding in the bottom of her waste basket.

Chilled from shock, Twila's body shivered convulsively as she struggled into bed. She pulled the covers over her head in an effort to cloak the humiliating nakedness she felt. Curled into a tight ball she wept bitter tears into her pillow. *No one will ever want me now. I'm spoiled, worthless. I should have been able to stop him.* Silent sobs racked her body. *What will my parents say? What will it do to the church?* Deep wrenching sobs tore from within her. Guilt and shame made her tremble uncontrollably. *The blood. What will happen if ...* Each tormenting thought forced another gut wrenching sob from her.

"Ron, look at this. Twila didn't even pick up in the kitchen." Emily sat her box of dishes on the kitchen counter and sighed as she looked over the clutter. "She's usually sitting up waiting to help put things away and to hear about everything."

"She must be pretty tired." From the entry hall he looked down the stairs. "Her lights are already off."

"Really? We're not even that late." Emily was already loading snack dishes into the dishwasher. "She must be really tired. I won't be long here and at least we won't have to stay awake until she tucks us in bed." Ron had already headed for their bedroom to watch the late evening news.

Late into the night, Twila lay exhausted. Her mind was numb. Only an occasional dry sob shook her limp body. The horrible event of a few hours before seemed illusory, unreal, impossible. *I'll pretend it was a nightmare. No one will ever know. I won't tell.* Gradually her thoughts became convictions.

She had seen programs on TV where victims of rape were blamed. No one believed them, and justice wasn't done. If she told anyone it could only create more problems, hurt her mom, destroy her dad's ministry, the church. *There's really no reason to tell anyone.* Her mom would never have to be upset by knowing. Her dad could continue as pastor. The church wouldn't be upset. Who would believe her anyway?

One hour melted into another and Twila made her decision with deep resolve. As quiet and certain as the coming dawn, she vowed never to tell anyone she had been raped. *I won't think about it.* Already she refused to replay the details in her mind. She could forget. She would forget. It would all go away. No one would ever know.

Twila yawned as she slouched, half asleep, in the chair beside the kitchen table. She was glad it was Friday. The last four days of her life had been the longest she'd ever known and tomorrow she could sleep in.

"You look kind of tired, Twila, are you feeling all right?"

"Yeah, I just haven't been sleeping well this week." She wasn't about to say she'd had nightmares and woke up restless and unable to sleep. She stretched and pushed a straggling strand of hair from her face. "What time do you and Dad leave for Orlando?"

"This afternoon, and Kathy said she'll come over before supper. She's tired, too. I guess teachers get as tired as the students by this time of year. Three weeks are about all that's left now, and they'll go fast." Emily was pouring half-&-half into her second cup of morning coffee. "Grandmother will be here next week when we get back from revival. We'll finish your shopping for the prom then."

Emily noted Twila's indifferent shrug. When had she ever been so disinterested in shopping? And for her first prom? While Emily studied her daughter, she remembered the strong impression she'd had the day before. She and Ron had nearly finished their weekly hour of prayer together in the church prayer room when she had had such a strong impression to spend more time with Twila. Emily mentioned it to Ron later that evening on their way home from church. "I just can't explain it, Hon, but I feel so strongly that I need to make Twila my number one priority this summer."

On Saturday morning before breakfast, JoAnn stood surveying the empty nursery. "John, I've decided on using Winnie the Pooh characters. I want white ceilings and walls, then we'll paint little groupings, and use Eeyore and Tigger, and Christopher Robin and the whole bunch."

"Who's the artist?" John smiled at her creative ideas.

"Me. I'll get some carbon paper, a coloring book and a few little cans of paint." She shrugged and smiled. "Any reason why I can't do it?"

Twila hesitated in the hallway, holding her few remaining purchases for the prom. She had felt secure enough having Kathy staying with her while her parents were in Florida. Sleeping in her parents' bed had helped overcome the nightmares and she felt more rested.

Now, with her parents home and her grandmother visiting, she had to go down to her own room. Nights were the worst. Every twig that scratched her window and every cry from a prowling cat made her shudder. Sleep escaped her as she lay alone, crying, trying to forget. Vague, unsettling dreams often disturbed what little sleep she did get. One sleepless night, she thought of a solution.

"Mom," she said as the two of them drove home from taking Emily's mother to the airport. "Now that Grandmother's gone, why don't I just move up to the guest room and that way you and Dad won't have to run the air conditioning downstairs?"

"Twila, are you sure you'd be happy in that little bedroom? You have so much more room downstairs." Emily said nothing of her surprise at having a mature, intelligent child, wanting to conserve energy. She knew from Dawn and Joey that teens often bounced between childish immaturity and logical adult thinking. She simply wasn't ready for such conservative thinking from Twila and smiled to herself, only vaguely aware of a disturbing tug somewhere in the back of her mind. Did she imagine that Twila avoided being downstairs without her or Ron?

Every morning Twila counted the weeks on her calendar again and again. She'd never skipped — something was wrong. She glanced around her new, little room and thought of her own big inconsistency. All her clothes were put away and her dresser neat but the bed remained unmade. Not only was she running late again, she didn't have the energy to make it. Besides, she had other things on her mind.

Could the memory of the rape experience be making her so tired? Twila refused to think about that night. She shrugged, helplessly. There were so many reminders. Whenever she had to go downstairs, especially at night; when she saw newspapers on the news stands; when she heard lectures in health class at school. She'd always argued against abortion but ... what if?

Every night, it seemed, there was more about the abortion debate, the Supreme Court's coming vote to determine the constitutionality of a Missouri statute regulating the performance of abortion. She wanted to cover her ears at night when her dad watched the news, or leave the room when her parents would discuss the abortion issue.

"The pro-choice advocates make such a big deal about the times a mother's life is at stake and what's that, less than two percent of the cases?" Ron had turned down the sound on the commercials while he waited for the sports. "That and cases involving rape and incest."

Emily wasn't interested in sports but she'd finished writing her mother a letter and joined Ron in the living room for the rest of the news. "I'm afraid in most cases abortion's a quick fix for an inconvenient pregnancy. I can't imagine how a woman must suffer when she finally begins to realize what she's done. No matter what the circumstances, it's still a human life that God created."

Twila heard them talking from the kitchen. She agreed with them, but what about her situation? What would it do to her dad, and the church? Her mother would just die. Just thinking about it made her tired. That's probably why she was so exhausted all the time, she reasoned. She'd be glad when it would all just go away.

Twila checked her purse to see if she still had some Vivarin. *I've got to stay awake for finals today.* She grabbed her swimsuit and books, took a Coke from the refrigerator and left for school. "Swim team after school tonight, Mom. Jeff will bring me home afterwards."

Jeff Hanson was planning to go to Harvard in the fall and study law like his father. His maturity and his thoughtful ways appealed to Twila and the two had become good friends while on the swim team together. They respected each other's opposite views on religion and life while they enjoyed a friendship free from the usual fears and risks associated with dating. Other than swim team, they moved in different circles. Maybe that's why Twila felt she could trust him with her problem.

"Jeff, I need to talk to you, but you've got to promise not to tell anyone."

"Why sure, Twila. Lay it on me."

"Don't tease, I'm serious." Her voice was sharp, tense. It caught Jeff's attention. He noticed her pensive expression, so unlike the usual Twila, always the life of the party.

"Heavy stuff, huh?" Tender now, the "boisterous buddy" stuff gone, he sat silent and waited. He saw how she huddled next to the door, so still, staring straight ahead. He sensed her struggle. Caring and gentle he asked, "Twila, you all right?"

"I was date raped." Date rape sounded more believable than just saying rape, Twila reasoned, even though most of her friends knew she couldn't single date until she was sixteen.

Jeff took a deep breath which he blew out slowly through his tightened lips. "Are you pregnant?"

Twila shrugged.

"Have you told anybody?"

"I don't have the heart to tell Mom, it would upset her too much and I can't tell Dad. Just think what it would do to him."

"You're not leaving yourself many options." Jeff waited a moment, wondering what he should suggest, what he should do. "How do you feel about abortion?"

Twila shrugged again.

"Well, what we need to do first is to find out if you really are pregnant. Maybe you're worried about nothing."

"I don't know where to go and I can't drive to get there if I did."

"I think there's a crisis pregnancy center in the mall. Let me check it out this afternoon and I'll take you tomorrow after school."

"But someone will see me."

"No, it's upstairs along with a bunch of other offices."

Twila said nothing to Jeff when she stepped out of the inner office of the pregnancy center and hurried to the door. Jeff had to walk fast to keep up with her as she ran quickly down the mall stairs. She said nothing until they were settled inside the car.

"I've never lied before."

"What do you mean?"

"I didn't give them my real name."

"Under the circumstances you…"

"I couldn't give them my name. They'd know who I am. Everyone knows we're the only Herrods in town and they'd automatically know who my dad is, so I lied. It's wrong to lie." Twila sighed heavily. "Anyway, it's not conclusive."

"So you still don't know anything?"

Twila shook her head. "They wanted to talk to me about an abortion. Jeff, there's no way I could have an abortion in there. Dad's too well known, and if the wrong person ever found out…"

"Didn't you say your folks are going out of town?" Twila nodded. "We'll skip school and I'll take you to Tulsa. I can go anywhere I want as long as I show up at a reasonable time at night. My parents never ask questions."

"But it's $300." Huge tears spilled down Twila's cheeks. She sniffled and wiped them away with the back of her hand. "I can't afford it."

"I can," Jeff volunteered, more concerned than wise about helping his trusting friend. "My parents never ask how I spend my money. They'll never need to know."

"I don't know…"

Then Jeff's mother stumbled across a note of Twila's discussing their plans. Jeff explained over the phone, "Twila, they're not angry or upset. It's just that since you're a minor, from a legal standpoint it could create a real problem."

"Oh, I'm sorry. I didn't even think about that." Twila's feelings were mixed. Part of her mind was in panic, but at the same time a sense of relief washed over her. She didn't have any idea what she would do next — but at least it wouldn't be an abortion. She felt peace.

O h, look! There is Emily, praying again. Praaaayer! Praaaayer! Praaaaayer! Emily's faaaaithful praaaayers answered before she even knows what she's praying about. There's always the danger of His immediate response to prayer.

Without realizing it, her prayer has protected the grandchild she doesn't even know exists. The baby is safe for now. But even her praaaayers won't stop the natural chain of events already begun — nor their consequences.

Emily's burden to spend time with her daughter became more pronounced and she made opportunities to be with Twila. When Eva Morris, a friend and respected church member, invited Ron and Emily to dinner, Emily asked, "Eva, would you mind if we bring Twila? I've been impressed to make her my first priority this summer. If she'll come, that is. You know teenagers."

"Oh, by all means. We'd be delighted to have her."

Emily stepped into Twila's room. "Eva Morris has asked Dad and me over for supper next Thursday evening. Do you want to go with us or would you rather get a pizza and stay home?"

"I'll go."

"She's already said you're welcome to join us, but I want you to understand she's inviting some others. Dad and I will be the only ones under sixty."

Twila didn't change her mind.

Emily turned back to her room. *This is neat. Maybe the Lord has impressed Twila to spend time with me.* Still, Emily couldn't shake the impression that something was wrong. Everytime she went anywhere, Twila shadowed her. Emily loved her company, but couldn't ignore the fact that her daughter was pulling away from her friends. Or were her friends shying away from her? Either way, for Twila, it was simply not natural.

June - July 1989

I t was eleven before Twila woke up and even then it was Emily that got her stirring. "Twila, I'm going to run some errands, do you want to go along?"

"Is Dad home?" Twila stifled a yawn and tucked a strand of hair behind her ear as she made her way to the refrigerator for a coke.

"Well, no, Sweetheart. Dad's already gone to the church."

"I'll go then. Give me a minute to pull some clothes on."

"Tell you what, Twila," Emily said as they pulled up to a stop sign a short time later. "Let's drop these clothes off at the cleaners first, then we'll go by McDonald's for a Happy Meal for lunch before we finish our errands.

"Mother, what would you do if I was pregnant?" Twila's unexpected question startled Emily and she hesitated at the stop sign longer than necessary before she answered.

"Well, Twila, we'd just go on with life and do the best we could."

I t was a warm June night when Eugene again ambled aimlessly to the end of his dark street and walked up the slight, weed-covered incline. Below him, on Interstate 540, the world sped by. Cars with people all going someplace. Eugene felt trapped.

The familiar feeling of abandonment crept over him and he wandered back down the street, hands jammed in his pockets. For a long time he stood silently in the dark shadows of the trees. He felt deserted. He always felt so — so nothing. So much less than — than what? Echos of his childhood clamored in his mind. His uncle's gentle taunting, "Be a man." "A man," his dad had growled so often. "Be a man," his mom had screamed repeatedly before she'd turned against him.

Memories kindled in his mind and smoldered as he stared at his house, pictured every room and recalled the pain-filled scenes. A screen door slammed. Eugene saw the light go on in Betty's house next door. *Wonder where she's been. Nice woman, when I've worked for her. Come to think of it, that's the only time she talks to me, when she wants something. She just uses me. She doesn't like me. No one likes me.*

The only remaining light in Betty's house flicked off. *Her bedroom light. She's alone in her bedroom.* The need to reassert his strength began to permeate his thoughts. He needed to feel powerful. To control a weaker being. He'd had it all before. He'd have it again.

E ven with sleeping-in every morning Twila seldom felt fully rested and on mornings when she was particularly tired she felt sick. The possibility she might be pregnant was becoming a genuine fear. She looked at her calendar again, thinking back. She counted the weeks. She counted the days. What would it be like to be bulging fat in front? She imagined the belittling stares, the sideways glances. She wondered who would believe her and who wouldn't. She kept thinking about her dad's reputation. She could hear the whispers. "Hey, you know the preacher at First Baptist, the big First Baptist? His fifteen-year-old daughter is pregnant."

And what about the baby? What would I do with a baby? I'll just keep it, she decided. *Other girls keep their babies. I can dress it and feed it and play with it.* Twila remembered Melanie Blake, a friend in Kenner. She had a baby boy and decided to raise him herself. *I can do it, too. Mom and Dad will help me.*

Las Vegas hosted the national Southern Baptist Convention in June 1989 and, like most years, the Herrods and Seaborns looked forward to some time together.

"We thought lunch in the mountains might be worth the drive — to get out of this heat." Ron had loosened his tie, and was laying his suit jacket over the back seat.

"Now, that sounds all right." Miles settled into the passenger's side of the Lincoln Continental. "Nice set of wheels you've got here."

"Sure is. My associate made reservations for a car but when we arrived there wasn't room for all of us and our luggage so we were given an upgrade at no extra charge." Ron had headed into the traffic, maneuvering into the lanes marked WEST.

"Not a bad deal, I'd say," Jeanne commented from the back seat.

"We sure didn't wipe any tears over it," Emily admitted.

Ron and Miles talked convention issues while Emily and Jeanne discussed family matters. "Well now, Emily, how are you doing after your surgery last winter? I understand that was a pretty major deal."

"Oh, I'm fine now, I guess, even though it was sorta one of those do or die emergency things." Emily laughed easily, making light of the ordeal. "My doctor said when he got in there he found my gall bladder is so bad it's going to have to come out before long."

"Not right away, I hope?"

"It'll be a couple of months yet before I get over the last surgery. I'd like to wait until fall and I get Twila back in school."

Over lunch the conversation centered around Ft. Smith. Ron spoke softly, his reedy voice barely audible above the hum of the restaurant. "The situation really bothers me. David, our son-in-law, had such a positive experience as youth minister at his previous church. Parents encouraged him, built him up, praised him for all the time and energy he gave their young people. He's doing the same things at Ft. Smith and is getting so little appreciation. It's the same opposition I feel toward most changes I suggest."

"You've got quite a challenge before you, Ron." Miles never thought in terms of problems. He listened intently as he crunched on the ice from his water glass.

"The church is growing statistically in attendance, baptisms and finances, but there is conflict there. We need a real revival. Part of the problem is that Ft. Smith has a small town mentality. With the exception of a few people, everybody's been born and raised right there. Anything different or anyone new becomes the topic of the town."

Ron shook his head. "I think the thing that bothers me the most is the effect it's having on my family. It seems every time the church staff is agreed on a new direction, some group opposes. It's creating tremendous stress on Emily.

Twila's aware of it, too. David and Dawn are discouraged. It's sad — really."

"Birchman did something new this year." Miles took another mouthfull of ice and chomped between words. "We brought in a group called Life Action from Buchanan, Michigan for a revival. They've got some 125 people on teams and all they do is go into churches and hold these meetings."

"We know about them. Had a team of theirs ten years ago in Kenner. They made a real impact on the church. We had a revival that lasted for ten years."

"The team asked for two weeks," Miles explained, "but the church had so many things going they only set aside one. Then people started coming, started confessing bitterness, immorality, poor money management, unfaithfulness, you name it. People started getting right with the Lord. The church cancelled everything else and the Life Action team stayed for six weeks."

Ron was eager to know more. "Sounds like they might be a marvelous thing for Ft. Smith." Again, Ron hung his head and shook it. "There's just got to be something we can do to revive the Lord's work there."

As soon as he returned from Las Vegas, Dr. Herrod contacted Life Action headquarters and scheduled a week of meetings for the middle of October. Then he began urging people to pray for God to work in their church.

Two weeks before her sixteenth birthday, Twila sat Indian style in the middle of her bed, writing letters and adding notes in her calendar. The blinds were shut tight. Cassette tapes were scattered like an open fan to one side of the bed and Amy Grant's voice filled the room. It was late. Twila had long ago been to her parents' room to say good night. A smile crept over her face at the thought. How many years had she been "tucking them in?" It was a ritual she had slipped into gradually since she was usually the last to go to bed.

Twila looked at her calendar and counted the weeks again. It was June 24. *I'm six weeks late.* As nearly as she could remember, her mom and dad had been at the church that night eight weeks ago. *No! No! No! I just can't be pregnant. I just can't be.* She turned off her light, curled into a ball and cried.

Twila pushed the thought from her mind, choosing rather to believe it was the trauma of that night and her worry about being pregnant that interrupted her regular cycles and made her so tired. *After all, I don't have morning sickness unless I get up early. A lot of things could be wrong. The pregnancy test wasn't positive.* Twila ignored the fact that it had been weeks since she'd had it done. *I'll wait until I have some pain or get sick.*

No sooner would Twila convince herself she wasn't pregnant than she'd think about what she'd do if she did have a baby. *I'll just keep it. Babies aren't hard to take care of and they're so much fun and they sleep most of the time. It can sleep in my room. I can dress it and feed it and play with it. Mom and Dad will help me, and Dawn and David.*

"Twila." Emily's head was cocked slightly and a slight wrinkle of concern crossed the bridge of her nose. "Have you decided what you're going to wear tonight?" She'd turned from the kitchen sink, potato in one hand and peeler in the other.

"Well, no, not really." She had just crawled off the couch in the den and was stifling a yawn.

"Twila, what's gotten into you. Here I thought you'd be all excited and carrying on. Child, it's your sixteenth birthday!"

"I know, Mom. It's just that," she shrugged. "Oh, I dunno."

"Sweetheart, what's gotten into you?" Emily's New Orleans drawl became even more pronounced as she gently prodded Twila. "Your daddy's been looking forward to taking you out to dinner for weeks and you don't seem to care at all."

"Well, I do, Mom," Twila answered listlessly, but her eyes held no luster and her shoulders drooped. "It's just that I don't know what to wear." Twila dropped into the nearest kitchen chair and sighed.

"You what?" Such a comment was totally unlike Twila. "Twee Dee, you never have trouble deciding what to wear. You always plan your clothes days ahead for a special event and have them laid out the night before. Just wear anything you're comfortable in. Hurry, Sweetie. Daddy's probably on his way home from church right now. You know he doesn't like to be kept waiting."

When Ron and Twila returned from dinner, Emily had the family room decorated and full of friends. Twila barely managed to be polite and soon settled on the couch, passive and withdrawn. Joey noticed her unnatural silence and later commented to his mother.

"So what's with Twila? She's quiet. Very quiet. Twila's never quiet." Joey habitually spoke in jerks, as if each statement were individually thought out. "She's always making noise. She's like you, Mom. She talks to the dog. She talks to the frying pan. She talks to herself."

"Well, she sure didn't talk tonight." Emily carried the leftover cake upstairs and Joey followed with the party plates and cups. Setting things on the kitchen counter, she turned to her son. "I don't know, Joey, Twila is just not herself lately. When Daddy and David had revival meetings last month in Oklahoma, Dawn and Twila and I went along and we all stayed a couple of extra days at the resort. All she did was lay around the pool and sleep. Just stayed right close to us the whole time." Emily busied herself sorting through the birthday clutter, throwing away paper plates, plastic tableware, and putting food away. "She was the same way over the Fourth of July."

"She break up with somebody?"

"She hasn't really even started dating. She has these dark circles under her eyes and she looks so — unhappy. She didn't even get excited tonight about her presents."

Later Emily confided to Ron. "I think I'm actually angry." Ron dropped his paper only a couple of inches at Emily's remark. "The party had only been going on a couple of hours when she came upstairs and asked, 'Mother, when are they going to leave and go home?' When she said that I thought, 'You ungrateful child, I've gone to all this expense, all this food.' Ron, she knows she can't ask her guests to leave."

Ron's silence was something Emily had grown accustomed to during their 25 years of marriage. A silence she'd learned meant neither indifference nor lack of caring. If he had had an answer, he would have shared it.

Two days after Twila's birthday, Ron, Emily, David and several professional men left for a missionary trip to Brazil. Anticipation ran high for Dr. Larry Hyde, dentist Dr. Ken Hamilton, and the other men as they waited in Miami's International Airport for their delayed flight to Rio de Janeiro. There were fifteen in the group.

Ron, as usual, found it hard to wait and he intermittently paced the airport corridors and glanced furtively at his watch. From time to time different members of the group engaged him in small talk. Dr. Hyde found it interesting that Emily seemed to have the most soothing effect on her husband.

When the flight was finally called, the mission team from Ft. Smith took rows of seats to themselves for the nine-hour flight ahead. Once the seatbelt lights were off, Emily started walking down the aisle. "Larry, we're so happy you could get time away from your practice to come along." Emily knew the doctor only as an OB/GYN and a member of their church. He nodded warmly and she sat down in one of the empty seats. "Too bad your wife couldn't come along."

"Well, our house is kind of a mad house. Never know on a given day how many kids are going to be there." His speech was unhurried and his smile almost self-conscious. "With the baby and all, we've got quite a bunch to keep track of."

"I don't even know how many you have."

"Well, we've got so many coming and going, I'm not sure which ones to claim, but at last count, five. The oldest are boys. They're 21 and 20. And three adopted girls, 12, 11 and 3."

"Why did you adopt your girls?"

"My wife, Barbara, worked as a pediatric intensive care nurse. We were foster parents and our first two, Amy and Sarah, needed skilled nursing care. After we had them three or four years we just decided to adopt them. Kathleen's mother, we were told, was single, starved for love and the father wouldn't have anything to do with her or the baby once he found out."

"It's a miracle Kathleen wasn't aborted."

"Law's sort of a schizophrenic thing these days. If a girl's 12 or 13, she's an adult as far as pregnancy's concerned. She can go in without her parents' permission and terminate her pregnancy. Anything else, a doctor has to have permission to treat."

"I wonder if in 1979 the Supreme Court would have had any idea of the magnitude of their decision."

"How many people did? In truth, though, the first shots fired in the battle for abortion in this country were earlier than that. They started in the state of New York in 1967-68, and in Kansas in 1969 when the state laws changed. At that time it was a state law question."

"I don't believe I've ever heard all that before." Emily's interest was obvious.

"I talked to our pastor back then, but like a lot of other Christian leaders at that time, he hadn't studied the abortion issue at all, so I didn't get any insight from him. I tried to determine on my own what the Bible said, but the word 'abortion' isn't in a concordance. At the time, I just went along with it."

"What changed your convictions?"

"For Barbara, my wife, it was simple. It was wrong. It wasn't until I looked up the words 'child' and 'womb' in the Bible that I realized the Greek word, βρεφοσ, or newborn, is the same word for unborn. I believe that in the mind of God, a child in the womb is as precious to Him as the newborn is to us or the grandparents.

"What's hard for the guys doing OB now, is the trend toward harvesting fetal tissue for therapeutic reasons. You get kids with severe birth defects and there is going to be pressure in the future to say 'let these kids grow and keep them alive so we can harvest organs.' It's going to be a real zoo."

Emily looked at the doctor, "That is really nothing less than child sacrifice, isn't it?"

Dawn stayed with Twila while their parents and David were in Rio. For the first few days, Melanie, a friend from Kenner, and her son, Christian, visited them. Their families had been friends for years and the girls all looked forward to seeing each other. Both Dawn and Twila enjoyed the antics of Melanie's chubby little toddler. Twila secretly observed how much work it was to keep up with him, how much time he needed. The dirty diapers, fussing when he was tired, always into things, up at night.

"Do you date much, Melanie?" Twila asked one night after they'd gotten Christian in bed.

"No," Melanie smiled wistfully. "To tell you the truth, there aren't many men my age out there who are interested in dating a mother of a two-year-old son. Besides, Mom's tired after chasing him all day while I'm at work, so I need to be home."

For Twila, the realities of single parenting began to take on a new meaning. *I'd never be able to keep up with a baby and finish school. Melanie hasn't finished high school. It wouldn't be fair to Mom and Dad.* She finally decided Dawn and David could take her child.

Twila, Melanie and Christian all slept in Ron and Emily's bed. They watched TV and talked late. Melanie would get up and take care of Christian in the morning, then go back to bed.

"Twila, I could really use some help." It was 10:30 a.m. when Dawn leaned against the doorframe of her parents' bedroom.

"Dawn, I'm so tired. Just let me sleep a little longer."

"But Twila, I've got to get some moving done and there's one more load of laundry to wash, plus clothes to fold. If you'd do that, it would help so much."

Dawn and David had sold their home some distance away and were moving into a rental house closer to the church. Several friends had helped them move all the big pieces and she was spending her time moving small items and unpacking while David was gone. Dawn also felt the pressure of Vacation Bible School only a couple of weeks away and wanted to get settled before then. The help she'd expected from Twila simply wasn't happening.

"Melanie," Twila mumbled to her friend next to her in Ron and Emily's bed, "I'll watch Christian if you'll go down to the laundry, put the last load in the dryer and bring up the folding." Twila reached for a piece of candy on the bedside table and popped it in her mouth.

"Twila."

"I can't believe you." Once in awhile Dawn could get exasperated.

"Oh, you mean the clothes? Melanie doesn't mind going downstairs, do you Melanie?" Twila did anything to avoid going downstairs, especially now, with her parents gone.

Dawn had unpacked enough so that by the time Melanie and Christian left, Dawn slept in her new home with Twila. The house had one main floor with a small finished attic.

"You can sleep in the attic room, Twila. There are boxes all over but you can make up the bed."

"No, that's too much trouble, I'll just sleep with you or get a pillow and blanket and sleep on the couch."

W hat'sssss wrong, Twila? Doesn't motherhood seem sooo glamorous, anymore? Not when there is a sniveling, demanding brat around all day.

Noooo more high school. Noooo college. Noooo dates.

You doooon't want a baby. You doooon't want to be pregnant. Why noooot get rid of it. A quick fix. It's legal. There's noooo reason your life should be disrupted. Surely, you could figure some way to have an aboooortion.

July 30 —
August 1, 1989

Twila awoke slowly and tried hard to ignore her mother's call. "Twila, Sweetie, if you don't get up, you won't be ready to go when Dad leaves for church."

"I know." Her sleepy voice never reached past her bedroom door. *I wonder if pregnant women feel tired. But I'm still not sick in the mornings. I just can't be pregnant.* Twila argued with herself. Slowly she rolled over and sat on the side of her bed. *It's got to be something else that's wrong.*

For three months she'd tried to ignore the clear evidence of her condition. Standing at the bathroom sink, while waiting for her hair rollers to heat, she splashed cold water on her hot, teary face. Thoughts of school raced through her mind. Registration was only three weeks away. If she really was pregnant, it was time to face facts. It was time to stop nursing the fear and humiliation that had tormented her for three long months.

Determined, she flung aside the fear that had been paralyzing her for so long, and began to rely on her own natural ally, logic. Pulling on the clothes she'd laid out the night before, she decided she had to talk to someone, and started down a mental list of names.

Mom? Twila shook her head. Her mother had had one major surgery and was scheduled for another in just two weeks. *Dad?* Twila couldn't even imagine how her father would handle it, and the thought of what it would do to his reputation. Would people at church even believe she had been raped? Without a doubt, the pregnant teenaged daughter of the pastor of Ft. Smith's largest church would give the town gossips a tasty morsel to savor.

"Ready, Twila?" She could hear her dad close his office door. She stepped into her shoes, grabbed her Bible and purse from her bureau, poked a hair bow between her lips and ducked back into the bathroom. Grabbing the wet face cloth, she dabbed her eyes again, tucked her curler box under her arm, grabbed her makeup bag, and dashed up the stairs into the kitchen.

With the dexterity of a normal teen, Twila added a diet Coke to her Sunday morning necessities. "See ya later, Mom." She called in the direction of the master bedroom, and headed out the door.

"Good morning, Knothead." Twila settled into the front seat beside her dad. "Ready as usual, I see."

Twila felt comforted by her dad's warm smile and relaxing banter. She dropped her bow from her mouth into her lap. "I'm always ready on time, Dad, you know I am," she sputtered, knowing full well he welcomed her company, curlers and all. For her, riding to church early with her dad was simply a means of having more time with her friends.

As usual, Ron prayed aloud as he drove the short distance to church, while Twila pulled the rollers from her hair and listened. "Our Father, thank You for the opportunity to serve You today. Thank You for the privilege of worshiping You. I ask for renewal in the hearts of Your people here this morning. Give me Your anointing as I speak today and may Your name be glorified, I pray. Amen."

Twila applied her make-up and finished fixing her hair in the private bathroom off her father's office. She savored the cozy, privileged feeling she enjoyed there each Sunday morning. Being one of the first kids to reach the youth department gave her the opportunity to visit briefly with which ever teacher arrived early. Mrs. Plummer was always among the first.

"Morning, Ms. P," Twila greeted from across the nearly empty hall. Carolyn Plummer waved her greeting and smiled warmly. *Of course. Ms. P.* Without a second thought, Twila threw away the mental list of names she'd been compiling earlier.

The noisy mix of over eighty happy adolescent voices bounced off the walls, filling the youth assembly hall with the usual Sunday morning sounds. Before the department director started the singing, Twila wove herself through the maze of kids and stopped directly in front of Mrs. Plummer.

"Ms. P, I've got to talk to you."

Mrs. Plummer noted an unusual note in Twila's voice and the heaviness in Twila's eyes suggested something serious.

"Okay, Twila. We have time before classes start. Let's just go to my classroom now." Twila followed. Without intrusion, Carolyn watched as Twila closed the door tightly and pulled two chairs aside. They sat together, facing each other.

"Ms. P, this is very serious."

"Okay, Twila. Are you all right?"

"Yes and no." Twila looked down at her hands and toyed with her fingernails. "Ms. P, I'm pregnant."

Twila, you're the least likely person. I know you're open and flamboyant and enjoy the admiration of young men, but I can't believe this. "Is this through a relationship?"

"No." Twila's face crumpled and tears began to roll down her cheeks. "I was raped." Carolyn stood and put her arms around Twila. Then they both cried.

"I'm so sorry, Twila, so very sorry." Carolyn fought for her own composure before she could trust herself to speak again. "I love you."

"Ms. P, I'm so scared. I don't know what to do."

"Are you sure you're pregnant?"

"Yes, ma'am."

"Did he threaten your life?"

"Not in words, but I was terrified."

"Do you want to tell me about it?" Carolyn sat down again facing Twila and holding her hands. Before Twila spoke she pulled back and looked around the room.

"Ms. Plummer, it happened one night about three months ago when I was home alone ... "

Mrs. Plummer listened, stunned and amazed, as Twila stoically recalled the incident.

"Did he say anything at all to you during that time or after? Any kind of threats? Anything?"

"No. He never said a word."

"Was it someone you know?"

"No."

"What did he look like?"

"I didn't really look at him, but I think he was about five feet seven or eight."

"What was he wearing?"

"It seems like he had on blue slacks and I know he was wearing a plaid shirt, a blue plaid. And he was clean. He was very clean cut."

"Twila, why didn't you tell someone?"

"I just didn't want to talk about it. I didn't think I would get pregnant and I know —" Twila started to cry again. "I just know I am."

"But why didn't you tell someone that night?"

"I didn't want my mom and dad not to trust me."

Carolyn handed Twila a tissue, took both of Twila's hands in her own and looked directly into her troubled face. "I'm going to tell you just what I would want someone to tell my daughter, if that had happened to her. You must tell your mother. She loves you more than you will ever know." Ms. Plummer, began to cry again and wiped her tears as she talked.

"It hurts me to know this has happened to you. We're good friends, but Twila, if you were Alice, I'd want to know every detail so that I could take care of you. There are so many things that could happen to you now, things that could be damaging to the future." Carolyn, spoke with careful emphasis. "You need care. Now. I'll go with you."

"No, Ms. P." Twila pulled her hand away and shook her head insistently. "I can't tell her now."

"Twila, you cannot wait any longer. You need to tell your mother. Now."

"But I can't now, there are too many things going on now. There's Bible school this week and she's got surgery coming up and all and she doesn't need this. I don't want to worry her with it now." Twila kept shaking her head, her voice emphatic with desperation. "Ms. P, this will really upset my mom."

"Rightly so." Mrs. Plummer waited a moment for the tension to ease before taking another tack. "Then tell Dawn. Tell Dawn now. You need care from family. Twila, I love you more than anything, but I cannot love you the way your mother does. She needs to be able to care for you now as much for her sake as for your own.

"Twila, I can tell you right now she's not going to love you less and she's not going to blame you. I know your parents well enough to know there's not enough threat here for you to be frightened of their reaction." Carolyn waited a moment again, before going on.

"Then tell Dawn. Promise me you'll tell Dawn. Twila, you need a pregnancy test to verify this. You may not be pregnant."

"Yes. I am. I've thought of abortion. And I've thought of keeping it, and I've thought of adoption. I know that I don't want to get an abortion. This baby has a right to live." Twila's eyes held both fear and sincerity and tears spilled down her blotched face. She shook her head and softly cried. "It's not this baby's fault — the circumstances." She cried quietly.

"I know I'm not ready for this responsibility and it isn't fair for my parents to have this responsibility again — not being their child."

Carolyn, slowly absorbing the horror of Twila's ordeal, observed the quiet control of the child-mother and marveled at the way Twila had thought through and dealt with her circumstances in her own mind.

Carolyn asked the one question that burned uppermost in her thoughts. "Twila, how have you dealt with this? How have you carried this tremendous weight — this — what happened to you? How have you handled this all this time by yourself?"

"Well, I cried a lot. I washed my face and went to bed. I just curled up and I cried. I did that a lot. I'm okay now. It's just that I feel real afraid."

"Afraid?"

"To make the right decision, to do what's right. I just don't know what to do next."

"You need to tell your mother. Let her help you with those decisions. You need medical care, Twila, it's so important." Carolyn began sharing some reasons for prompt medical care for the baby's sake as well as Twila's. As she talked, the color drained from Twila's face.

"I'm going to be sick." Twila was fanning herself. "I'm going to throw up." She headed for the door. "I'm going to throw up." Mrs. Plummer followed her to the rest room.

"Here, let me help you." Carolyn took a wet towel and cleaned a few strands of Twila's hair, and gave her another towel to freshen her face.

"Do I look just awful?"

"Well, you look like you've been throwing up." Twila smiled weakly. "Twila, it's just about time for classes to start. I'll have my class go with another one and we can talk to your mother."

"No, I'll tell her. Within the next two weeks, I'll tell her."

"Twila, you don't need to wait that long."

"I'm going on over to my Dad's office now and I'll just lay down until I feel a little better."

"Are you sure this is what you want to do?"

"Yes."

Carolyn stood and watched Twila walk away. *Not a word about her own pain. She didn't even ask, "Why me?" I can't believe how grown up she is.*

"I cried, I cried a lot." Mrs. Plummer kept hearing those words. *Could it be that during all those lonely nights that Twila cried, the little girl-teenager was being pushed aside and the young woman, needed to nurture this child, took over?*

As Carolyn walked to her classroom, she carried a weight of anguish and heartbreak for Emily. Twila said two weeks. Was that too long to keep her confidence? Carolyn wondered at what point would the Herrods feel she was withholding vital information? What would she want done if she were Twila's mother?

John and JoAnn were enjoying a Saturday afternoon in Forest Park. They each had a book, but they talked more than they read. All they had heard from the agency for almost a year was another letter restating how few babies were available. Other couples who had adopted continually advised, "Don't put all your eggs in one basket. Apply to three of four agencies and that way whoever has a baby first, you get it."

"I don't know what other agency I'd want to apply to."
JoAnn had put her book down.

"Can you live with possibly having to wait longer?"

"I don't want to wait longer, but I like the way Hope
Agency ministers to the birth mothers, and I really like their
contact policy. I guess I feel more secure with them." JoAnn
sighed deeply.

John nodded, signaling for JoAnn to see a squirrel
darting toward them. They watched in silence until
something startled the jittery creature and it scrambled up
the nearest tree.

"What did it take us, two and a half months to fill out the
adoption papers?" John reached over and picked up a fallen
maple leaf.

"Yes, at least, and if we start with another agency we've
got to start making their payments and going to their
meetings. John, we've already put a lot of time and money
into Hope."

"JoAnn, I have no doubt that in time God is going to give
us a child and I'm comfortable believing He can do that as
easily if we apply through one agency or a dozen."

Before the evening ended they mutually agreed to wait
longer.

T wila, we've got to go or we're going to be late." Emily
gathered up her Vacation Bible School lesson packet
for third graders, checked the lock on the front door and
headed for the garage. "I'll be in the car."

"I'm coming." It was one of those mornings Twila had to
get up early, and she felt nauseated. This was only the second
day of Bible School and her stomach already churned. *How
can I keep up with active five year olds and teach all week?*

Twila took one last look at herself in her full length mirror and her hands went to her waist. She remembered her promise to Mrs. Plummer. Already she couldn't wear some of her fitted clothes. Twila hoped she didn't look as pregnant as she felt when she hurried toward the kitchen. She grabbed a soda on the way out the door, hoping it would help settle her stomach.

Dr. Herrod had the usual morning greeting in the opening Bible School assembly. His enthusiasm infused the youngsters before they headed to their respective classes. Emily expertly settled her third graders and captured their attention as she told the story of Joseph, betrayed by his brothers and sold into slavery.

"Everything didn't go right in Joseph's life," she emphasized. "Satan intended it for evil, but God brought good out of it. Sometimes things don't go right in our lives, but we know for certain that God is ultimately in charge."

Strange. I feel as if the Lord is talking specifically to me through my own words. Emily had experienced the same awareness before but usually when she spoke to other women — not when she taught young children.

David's office opened off a main hall not far from the classrooms. He always kept his door open as an invitation for young people to walk in, so he wasn't surprised when Twila entered.

"Twila, how's class going for you this morning?"

"I dunno. I just walked out." She slumped down into the couch against the wall in David's office. "I've got a real problem, David. It's pretty private." David stepped out and made a brief statement to his secretary. When he returned, he closed his door. After he turned his chair, he sat down and faced Twila directly.

"Want to talk about it, Twila?"

"I'm pregnant."

David couldn't believe it of Twila. He'd worked with a lot of youth and been surprised more than once, but he never expected such words from his high-principled little sister-in-law.

"How did that happen?" David kept his voice even, casual, as if they were talking about a lost hair ribbon. He knew her parents' policy about dating, and that she didn't have a boyfriend.

"I was raped." Twila burst into tears and David sat dumbfounded, unsure how to respond. Aware of his own shock, and unable to believe how anything as unbelievable as rape could have happened, he sat silent. Rape wasn't supposed to happen to someone in his family and the sobbing girl in front of him was family, too innocent, too sweet, too fragile to be so broken.

Knowing it wasn't his place to comfort her as her father, David only scooted his chair closer and took her hand. "I'm just real sorry, Twila. I feel so bad for you." David was beside himself with compassion for her. "I'm so sorry." He kept trying to console her. He pulled a couple tissues from the box on his desk and tucked them in her hand. "This should never have happened to you, not to any woman. I understand how terrible you must feel but your family is going to stand behind you. Everybody's going to support you. I feel so sorry, so very sorry." Except for an occasional hiccuping sob, Twila stopped crying.

"Where did it happen?"

"At home. The guy must have been in the family room when I went downstairs to get ready for bed."

"Where were your parents?"

"Here — at the church. It happened around the first part of May."

"Did you know who it was?" David didn't want to prod too deeply but he did want her to know he cared and give her a chance to talk if she wanted to.

"No, I just know that he was a white man." She described what little she could remember about him.

"Have you told your parents?"

"No."

"Who does know?"

"I told Ms. Plummer last Sunday morning. She made me promise I'd tell Mom."

"Twila, are you sure you're pregnant?"

"Pretty sure."

Married women don't always know when they're pregnant. She's barely sixteen. I wonder how much she knows about physiology. She needs to talk to a knowledgeable woman.

"As far as the rape, Twila, I think you need to tell your parents as soon a possible, but as far as whether you're pregnant or not, let me have Dawn talk to you so that we don't just go straight up to your parents and drop this humongous bomb if we're not sure about it." She nodded. "But whatever we find out, Twila, you must understand that they've got to know."

"But I don't want to hurt them; they'll feel so bad about it. That's why I haven't told them. I — I feel so ashamed." Tears rolled again from her big blue eyes and David handed her another tissue from the box on his desk.

You dear, dummy. They'll understand and they'll feel for you and won't come down on you for anything like this. "Twila, if you can tell your parents, I think that would be best; if you don't feel you can do the initial announcement, then I will do it if you want me to. Or Dawn will, I know, if you'd feel better about having her do it, since she's a closer member of the family."

David looked at his watch. "It's nearly noon. Why don't I go and talk to Dawn, then I'll come back and take you over there. We'll see what Dawn says. Then if you want her to go to your Mom's, or if you want to go to your Mom, we'll just take it from there." Twila nodded.

"I'll come back here after Bible school's over, then?"

"That will be fine." David stood and went to the door. "Twila, your family is going to support you through this. I know they will."

As David drove the few blocks to his home he wondered how they'd ever prove rape since it had been so long since it happened. He thought of the church situation, knowing immediately how the malcontents of the church would pounce on the Herrods. The fact that it was a white boy — David could hear the talk, "Yeah, right, a white baby. She most likely was out on a date."

He found Dawn sitting in the middle of the living room floor folding clothes. David noticed she had things set out in readiness for the barbecue they were having that evening to thank the people who'd helped them move. He didn't waste anytime with a preamble.

"Stay seated, Honey, we need to talk and you need to hear this sitting down. Twila just came in my office and told me she's pregnant, that she was raped." Dawn stared at David, speechless, as tears began to well up in her eyes.

"B-but how? When?"

He relayed the few details he knew. "I didn't feel it was my place to ask a lot of details. I told her you'd talk to her." Dawn wiped her eyes and rallied to the sense of urgency. She needed to think clearly. There would be time to sort out her own feelings later.

"Well, yes, of course I'll talk to her." Dawn got up and began stacking the folded clothes neatly in the basket.

"I told her we needed to find out first if she was really pregnant."

"I've got to go shopping this afternoon anyway so I'll pick up one of those home-test kits."

"I told her she needs to decide today whether she's going to tell your parents alone or if she wants one of us to tell them."

Dawn moved in a daze after David left to get Twila. She tried to imagine how Twila must feel; how she would feel if she had been raped and thought she was pregnant. *The last thing I'd want is anyone acting hysterical. I'll stay calm. Twila will need me to stay calm.*

After Twila arrived, her sister asked a couple of basic questions. "David and I both think it would be best to find out first if you're really pregnant," she said. "How do you feel about that?"

"Okay, I guess."

"I'm going to out to get a couple of things for this evening. Do you want to go with me and get a home pregnancy test or wait here?"

"I'll go." Twila seemed relieved by Dawn's calm suggestion.

"I'll call Mother and tell her you're with me for the afternoon, okay?"

She nodded agreement.

The doubts Twila clung to were erased after she took the test. "Dawn, I'm pregnant."

"When do you plan to tell Mom and Dad?"

Twila shrugged.

"Mother said she'd be by after she runs some errands. She'll pick you up in time to get home and change before supper tonight."

"Okay, but I'm so tired, could I just sleep for awhile?"

"Yes, Twila, but you have to tell Mom." Dawn spoke with gentle insistence. "You can't wait another day."

It was 10:30 p.m., the Herrods had been home from the barbecue at Dawn and David's about an hour. Ron had gone directly to his office in the basement and Emily sat in her housecoat at the kitchen table, going through the pictures of the Brazil trip she'd just had developed.

"Mom?" Twila had just come out of her bedroom from changing.

"In the kitchen, Twee Dee." Twila sat down and Emily, used to listening and working at the same time, kept on writing.

"Mom, I've got to talk to you."

"Sure, Twila, sit down and we'll go through these pictures together and you can talk." Twila always talked so her request was nothing unusual.

"Mother, I need to talk to you about something serious. I have to tell you something really heavy."

"Okay, that's fine." The worst Twila ever had to say never really amounted to anything.

"You need to stay seated."

Emily pushed her pictures aside and folded her hands on the table wondering what was so "heavy" she had to stay seated.

Twila, as usual, started by stating the blatant facts.

"I'm pregnant."

Emily blinked, not sure she'd heard right. "Okay, tell me that one more time." Emily knew this was impossible because they never allowed their girls to single date until they were sixteen and Twila had only had one date.

"I'm pregnant."

"You're kidding."

"I'm not joking." As she spoke, Twila's face crumpled and she burst into tears. In that instant, impressions of the summer flashed through Emily's mind; Twila's listlessness, the dark circles under her eyes, her hesitancy to go down to her bedroom. Emily also recognized her strong urge to spend time with Twila must have come from the Lord. *God knew she needed me.*

Emily wept, too, as she pieced her memories together. All the signs. The tiredness. Emily didn't doubt for a minute her daughter's jolting declaration. When Emily gained a measure of composure she began to probe gently.

"Okay. Now Twila, you've got to tell me exactly what happened." A picture began to take shape in her mind.

"I was raped." Twila's words didn't fit. *Rape!* Another picture formed in her mind. *No, God. Not rape!* Emily could feel her whole world, her whole life crumble down around her. Her elbows were on the table and her hands held the weight of her head. She could feel the blood drain from her face and with it her strength. She felt weak. *Now God, You know! Why did you let this happen? Do you know who I am? Do you know I'm the pastor's wife at First Baptist Church and You know that I have always done things for the good?*

It seemed as if God had let her down. While Emily inwardly shook her fist in God's face and questioned Him, her heart broke for Twila. Always the mother, Emily reached out to hold her daughter, to console, to take her baby's pain for her own.

"When, Twila?" she cried. "Where did it happen?"

Between her sobs Twila repeated her story again, "... A man ... downstairs ... I think it was the night of the ladies' banquet at church. I tried, but I couldn't stop him. I tried to get away, Mom, but he hit me across the chest and knocked me down on the bed. I tried so hard to get away. I really did."

"Of course you did." Emily cried. *God, how could You let this happen? In our home, while we were at church, serving You?* Emily felt betrayed.

"It wasn't your fault," she comforted. "But why didn't you tell us? We would have helped you." Emily didn't blame Twila, but the need to blame someone grew as anger welled up inside her. She thought of vengeance, and longed for the power to kill.

"I felt so ashamed, so guilty." Twila's need refocused Emily's attention.

"Mom, I didn't want to upset you. I didn't want to hurt Daddy. I was afraid ... "

"Of course you were, Sweetheart." Again, fragments of Twila's unexplained behavior during the summer flashed through Emily's mind. Twila always staying close to home, withdrawing from her friends, moving into the small guest room, her sullen strange behavior at her birthday party.

"Are you sure you're pregnant, Twila?" Emily still couldn't imagine her baby, sixteen less than a month, pregnant.

"Dawn got me a home test today. I'm pregnant."

Abortion. For an instant the thought passed through Emily's mind, and in that instant, she identified with the millions of women who'd grasped at that straw. She knew it was wrong — but it was the easiest thing to do. *Wouldn't Satan love it if we chose abortion?* Emily knew in the end it was only a worthless straw. She cast the idea aside.

"Twila, we have to tell your daddy."

"I can't, Mom."

"I know, Sweetie. I will."

Emily pushed herself up from the table and pulled Twila to her. They held each other close through another wave of weeping before Emily kissed away Twila's tears, and steeled herself to go through the short hall, down the stairs and across the family room to Ron's office. He sat behind his desk writing a memo when she walked in.

"Ron, I've got to talk to you," she said as she leaned against his bookcase.

"Sure." It wasn't an uncommon thing for Emily to walk in and want to talk. Like Emily, Ron often busied himself as he listened, but when she didn't keep talking he looked up. Immediately he noticed her swollen red eyes and tear-streaked face. "Em?" Ron got up from his desk and went to her. "What's wrong?"

Emily started crying again. Ron took her hand and led her to the love seat. "Sit down, Em." He pulled her down beside him.

"Twila just told me she's pregnant."

111

Ron felt a million arrows stab his heart. Like Emily, logic told him it wasn't possible, but before he could speak, Emily broke the worst of the terrible news.

"She was raped." Emily was crying again. She could feel Ron struggle with his thoughts as he gripped her arms and searched her face.

Rape! It's too horrible. I can't believe it. Twila did lie about some grades once. She must be lying again ... to cover up.

"Who was it?"

"She doesn't know. She never saw him before."

"What did he look like?"

"She said he was neat and clean. He was dressed nice and he was sort of tall but she can't remember much."

"Did he threaten her? Did he hurt her? Where did it happen?"

"Here, in her old room — downstairs. She said he knocked her down on the bed."

"It can't believe it." Rape was too impossible for Ron to accept, and Twila's condition could have only one other cause. *How could she lie to us? How could she do such a thing? How could she? How could she embarrass us like this?* As Ron held Emily they cried together while his thoughts continued to race. *After all, I am the pastor of the First Baptist Church. I'm looked upon as a spiritual leader. My family is above this sort of thing. What will this do to our ministry, our outreach, the rest of our family? How could she?*

One harsh accusation after another bombarded Ron's thinking until conviction arrested his thoughts. *Vindictive. Self-centered. Proud. Even if she is guilty, my heart should be broken for my daughter before any of these other things.* Ron cried even more from conviction and repentance.

The phone rang and Emily stepped over to her husband's desk to answer.

"Hello? Yes, Dawn, she told me and I've just told Daddy." Emily could hardly talk. "I'll call you in the morning. Thanks, Dawn."

When Ron looked up, Twila stood just inside his office door. He noted her drooping shoulders, her disheveled hair, and puffy, tear-stained face. He saw her fingers twisting nervously as her haunted eyes timidly found his. He recognized guilt and humiliation, pain and fear and her need for him.

For a moment he sat stunned, feeling what she must have felt, thinking what she must have thought. Heartbroken, he went to her with open arms. No words were necessary for those few moments while they held each other and wept. Treasured moments when Twila basked in her father's unconditional and accepting love. Life-altering moments when Ron, accepted not only his daughter, but her humiliation, her pain, her fear.

After a time, with an arm still around her, Ron and Twila sat together on the love seat. Emily sat on the armrest. As they asked questions, Twila tried hard to remember the painful details she'd worked for three months to forget. As they talked, they checked the calendar and pinpointed the fateful night — May 1, the night of the banquet.

Heeee heeee heee! Did you see their reactions? Did you hear them quesssstion God? It's strange how Hissss loyal subjects assume their gooood works earn them immuuuunity from my schemes. After all, His own Son wasss vulnerable. In the end, of course, God used even that to Hisss advantage but sooo few of His followers make that connection. Instead, they become angry and paralyzed by bitternessss.

I relish with great anticipation the spiritual warfare the Herrods now face. Their grrreat fall! After all, who will believe Twila's story, anyway. Hah! Humans secretly delight in shocking, sordid, demeaning liessss about each other. Especially about spiritual leaders. The Herrods' influence is at an end. Soon, they'll trouble meeee no more.

August 2 —
September 4, 1989

For Twila, healing began when she admitted the reality of her rape, told her parents and felt the assurance of their love and acceptance. For the first time in three months she felt relieved of the burden of her guarded secret, confident of her parents' love and support to face the future. Her parents, she knew, would handle everything.

For Ron and Emily, the nightmare had only begun.

Thoughts of failure, embarrassment, concern for Twila, and desire for revenge consumed them both. "To think someone actually came into our house and physically knocked her down and ... " Ron was livid with anger. "If I knew where to begin looking, I'd go right now and ... " His words were only safety valves releasing the first pangs of emotional shock. In time, uncontrollable sobbing gave expression to pain too intense for words.

Emily fought her own battle. She was equally incensed at the unknown assailant and wanted to strike out, but where and at whom? Then she thought of Twila. "My baby," she cried. "Violated, and for three months not telling anyone. I can't imagine what she's gone through."

"Why wouldn't she tell us? Why couldn't she trust us?" Ron agonized, then he blamed himself. "This wouldn't have happened if we'd have been home. I should have had better locks on the doors. And the alarm system, why didn't I go ahead and have that alarm system installed?"

For a long time they sat, chilled by thoughts of failure, the silence broken only by their crying. Eventually, Ron stood up and by habit began turning off his office lights.

As they stepped together into the family room, scenes of Twila's ordeal flashed through their minds. They saw how easily a man could have entered the patio door. They felt a chill in the same shadows where he'd hidden. They walked where he had walked to enter Twila's bedroom.

The door stood ajar, and as they walked past, their eyes could not avoid seeing the spread askew on the bed. The whole atmosphere seemed defiled. "It's no wonder Twila insisted on moving up to the guest room," Emily said, bursting into tears again. They fled quickly up the carpeted stairs to the refuge of their own bedroom, closing the door behind them.

For a time, shock robbed them of the ability to even pull back the covers and get ready for bed. "I'm not deserving enough to be a father." Ron's words were barely a whisper. "I've utterly failed as a pastor."

"We've got to concentrate on what to do now," Emily countered, even though she felt dead inside. They sat immobilized until gradually their feelings gave way to questions. "What shall we do? Who do we tell?" Even after they did get in bed, sleep eluded them and they lay weeping, taking comfort in each other's arms.

As the night crept slowly by, Emily thrashed in her broken sleep while Ron paced the bedroom, roamed through the house and wandered down the drive in their back yard. At times, he'd fall to his knees and pray or give way to another paroxysm of inconsolable weeping. Although the night seemed unendurably long, the morning and its responsibilities came all too soon.

True to her nature, Emily focused on action. After she started coffee, she called Dawn. "Twila told us everything, Dawn. I can't face people today. I can't stop crying. You've got to take my Vacation Bible School class." Next, Emily placed a call for Doctor Hyde. When she finally reached him, she cried again. "We have an emergency, Larry. Twila's three months pregnant."

"Bring her to the back door of my office at noon," he calmly instructed. "I'll be the only one here and I'll let you in."

As Emily started her day with the only steps she knew to take, Ron burrowed deeper under the covers, wishing the day away. He was incapable of focusing beyond the horror and far-reaching repercussions of Twila's tragic situation.

He heard Emily bring him coffee and set it beside the bed. "I'm quitting. I'll quit everything I've ever done." Slowly Ron emerged from his cocoon of bedcovers, shielding his squinting and swollen eyes from the morning light. "I can't do it anymore. I would rather die."

"That's ridiculous," Emily countered, even though she felt the same way. "It happened — and we've got to go on. We can't give up."

The feel of a familiar cup, and the taste of hot, cream-laden coffee gave a soothing sense of familiar comfort. As the hot brew washed away his sleepiness, a well known verse surfaced in his weary mind: *"Preach the word; be ready in season and out of season ..."* The habit of obedience to a Will beyond his own forced Ron into action. His strength lasted until he finished leading the joint worship service in Vacation Bible School, then he returned home and collapsed again in bed.

Dr. Hyde opened the back door of his office and immediately recognized Emily's devastation, but directed his attention first to Twila. After he recorded her answers to his routine questions, he said, "Hop up on the table, Twila. At three months this little one should have a strong heart beat."

Doctor Hyde moved the cool stethoscope over her stomach, then handed her the ear pieces. Twila's eyes opened wide at the frightening wonder of the smooth, racing rhythm that filled her ears. "It's so fast," she said as she passed the earpieces to her mother.

Hesitant, Emily placed them in her ears. Unbelievable joy surged through her as she listened to each distinct heartbeat of her first grandchild. *No, God. This is not real. I'm somewhere else.* The moment was so thrilling, yet so terribly wrong. She blinked back the tears that distorted the beautiful, trusting face of her own innocent baby. Her daughter, too young to be married, too young to give birth, too young for the responsibilities of motherhood, too innocent to comprehend the realities of her weeks and months of pregnancy yet ahead.

Doctor Hyde saw the radiance of Emily's smile fade into tears and he gave her a moment to regain her composure. "Twila's in good shape and the baby seems fine. From the dates you've given me, we're looking at a due date near the end of January." The doctor paused a moment to make a final note in Twila's chart, then he looked up at Emily. "Now tell me, how are you doing?"

"I think I'm going to make it, but," she blew her nose and wiped her eyes again. "I don't know about Ron."

"Where is Brother Ron?"

"He's home in bed — and he won't get up." Doctor Hyde followed Emily and Twila home where they found Ron in the living room, uncharacteristically frumpled and tipped back in his recliner chair.

Doctor Hyde's practiced eye read the signs of depression and devastation and he pulled a chair up along side the leader he'd come to love. He'd witnessed the heartbreak of other parents in similar circumstances and he knew the added burden his pastor carried, the mind set of the church, the community. "You look about the way I'd feel if I were facing your situation," he empathized. Then he sat and listened.

In time, the doctor skillfully led Ron and Emily to think of options. "Twila can stay in your home or go someplace else. There are places all around the country where girls can go, live safely, get support and get help placing their children for adoption.

"A boarding home situation?" Emily asked.

"Yes, a home for unwed mothers that provides medical care."

Ron and Emily missed their usual Wednesday morning hour of prayer together in the church prayer room. They couldn't pray. Emily went to church with her husband that evening simply to avoid the questions that would be asked if she didn't make an appearance. Besides, she had to talk to someone. *A woman needs a woman. I've simply got to talk to another woman.* Kaay Gean came to mind. Dear Kaay whom Emily had come to love and recognize as absolutely trustworthy as well as wise and strong.

"She didn't come tonight," Paul Gean explained when Emily stopped him in the foyer. "She wasn't feeling too good and she has company coming to get ready for." Emily sat near the back of the church during the evening Bible study for as long as she could hold her tears back, then she left for Kaay Gean's home.

Janey Spencer, Ron's secretary, suspected something was wrong Friday morning when he asked her to call one of of the church leaders. "See if he can come in during his lunch hour and if he can, order a lunch for both of us, would you please?" Janey had their lunches waiting when the man arrived and she left for her own hour-and-a-half lunch break. She was surprised that their conference continued even after she returned.

After his visitor left, Ron remained in his office alone for a few minutes before he buzzed the intercom. "Janey, I'd like to talk to you. Have Kathy hold all our calls." Janey took her steno book into his office and sat on the divan, surprised that before Ron said anything, he began to cry. She waited, wondering what could possibly be so wrong.

"Twila is pregnant," he finally said, and as he explained about the rape, Janey cried, too.

"Twila didn't want to upset us, and she felt dirty and ashamed, that's why she didn't tell us sooner. Then she realized she had to."

It was some time before Janey left Dr. Herrod's office. She left through the back door and drove up Grand Avenue to Porta's and ordered two chocolate malts. "I figured we both needed something to help us get through the day," she said, handing Ron one of the malts. "Porta's is said to have the best shakes in town." He smiled his gratitude.

Jeanne Seaborn sat figuring a crossword puzzle while Miles finished watching the late Thursday night news. Just after the sportscast finished, the phone rang. Miles took his glass of ice to the kitchen phone. Jeanne heard her husband's friendly greeting change from his warm "Hello there, Brother Ron, how ya doing?" to a more subdued, "I'm sorry to hear that. Does she have a steady boyfriend? Is she generally open and truthful with you? Does she know who it was? Is her story consistent?"

Miles listened further and prayed with Ron before concluding his conversation. "You certainly have quite a challenge ahead of you, Ron. We'll be praying for you. Now, keep in touch."

Jeanne could guess from the conversation that Twila was pregnant. After her husband was off the phone, he filled her in on the details. She suggested, "I feel we need to offer to have Twila come live with us. It's something I really want to do."

Since the Seaborns' four children were grown with families of their own, Miles and Jeanne had considered selling their home and building a smaller one but their plans never seemed to work out. "Who knows," Jeanne concluded, "maybe the Lord kept us in this house just so we could make it available to Twila."

"I thought the same thing while I was taking to Ron, but I wanted to see how you felt first. Let's pray and sleep on it overnight," Miles suggested. "If we feel the same way in the morning, I'll call them back."

Jeanne woke the following morning with plans for redecorating the large front bedroom next to their own. She and Miles talked to their grown children, all living in the area, then Miles called Ron.

"We feel that God is telling us to invite Twila to stay with us. Our children can be a source of encouragement to her." When Ron didn't respond immediately, Miles continued, "We have a crisis pregnancy center associated with the church with trained counselors. They have a wonderful Christian doctor available, contact with adoption agencies here in Ft. Worth and the high school is nearby."

"It all sounds too wonderful, Miles, I hardly know what to say. Let me talk to Emily and Twila. Give us some time to pray about it." When Ron related the invitation to Emily, she immediately recognized God's provision.

"Don't you see, Honey, it will be in a pastor's home with a lifestyle much like her own."

J oAnn hadn't dared to call the Hope Agency since they'd told her she wasn't trusting the Lord. A few times Ted Watson called her and for an instant her heart would stick in her throat only to hit the floor a moment later when he said he only had a question or needed to verify a phone number or name spelling.

Near the end of August, she opened another letter from Hope and read,

As our fiscal year draws to a close, we felt it a good time to give you an update … We will place about forty percent fewer babies than in the previous three years. A recent article in the CHICAGO TRIBUNE reports there are thirty abortions in this country for every adoption.

We do have hope that we will be able to place a child with you, yet it might be well for you to explore other agency possibilities while your application remains with us.

"How do you feel about it?" John asked after JoAnn shared the letter with him.

"I still feel best with Hope because I really do want contact with the birth mother."

"So you're satisfied with waiting?"

"At least for now." Later that evening, she went to the door of the nursery. Winnie the Pooh and his comrades smiled cheerfully from their appointed places on the walls. She couldn't help but smile as she looked from one to the other but the little, blue rocker and the car seat beside it beside it emphasized the otherwise barren room. It was time, she decided, to go out and buy a cradle.

I t was Wednesday, August 9, eight days since Twila's confession shattered Ron and Emily's lives. "Twila, I'm meeting Daddy this morning for our prayer time together. Do you want to go along?"

"No, Amy Gean's taking Amy Nunley and me to the mall."

"Are you sure you want to go there, Sweetheart?" Emily's eyes teared as she talked.

"Oh, Mom, I'm fine. You'll get back before I do anyway so I won't be here alone." *I can't believe you and Dad are still bawling over what happened after all this time.* "Really, don't worry about me."

Emily cried as she got ready to leave for the church. *I've got to pray. I've got to pray with Ron.* As yet, they'd not been able to pray together.

Over the years, their weekly prayer time became an hour they dearly loved, yet when Emily walked into Janey's office to let Ron know she'd arrived, she cried again. "Janey, I feel like we've been robbed, to think that some stranger came in and took our baby's most precious possession. It would have been easier if Twila had gotten pregnant on a date, but not by this — this act of violence."

As Ron and Emily approached the twenty-four-hour prayer room door, their feelings were mixed. Both of them knew the presence of God and longed for the sweetness of their prayer time together, yet at the same time they felt so much anger. Why had God allowed this to happen? Why hadn't He protected their daughter?

They were both aware that rumors were spreading throughout the congregation. If they could have, they would have gone off somewhere and died.

The Bible lay open before them as they knelt on the kneeling bench, and their eyes fell on an underlined verse, "Be anxious for nothing but in everything by prayer and supplication ... "

I can't worry about everything. I can't be anxious for anything. Emily let the truth of the words sink deeply into her mind.

" ... by prayer and supplication, with thanksgiving, let your requests be made known to God."

Ron had preached on the familiar text. He and Emily both knew God required a thankful heart as the condition of His promise.

"I'm not thankful," Emily spoke aloud. "I'm not." She struggled with the logic of God's command. *Now, Emily, you know it's not for you to feel; thanks is something you give.* Finally Ron and Emily said, "Okay." Emily cried as she prayed aloud.

"God, You know I don't feel it. I don't feel it inside, but the very best that I can tell You is, I am thankful. I am thankful that my daughter was — raped." Emily paused before she could say the horrid word. It felt like a knife in her throat as she spoke it "— and that she's pregnant ... " Within minutes, Emily felt as though she'd been transported from a dark valley to a place of peace where the Father impressed her with His promise that He would make her feel thankful.

Ron, too, obediently expressed thanks. "Forgive me, too, Lord for my anger toward You for allowing this unthinkable situation. It seems so wrong, but I choose to believe that this too, will work out for good. Use it Lord, and help us move ahead in the ministry, regardless of the circumstances. And Lord, I personally would ask for a grandson, but regardless, I commit this baby to You for your service."

Once Ron and Emily had obediently offered thanks to God, they could pray beyond themselves and begin praying for Twila that she could forget the details of the assault, forget the face of the stranger and be strong and wise in the months ahead. They also prayed for their grandchild and the couple who would adopt him. "Give him Christian parents who will raise him and lead him to You, Lord, we pray."

Although Ron did not experience the overall sense of peace in the same way as Emily, their prayer time together became a pivotal point as they began to evaluate their circumstances more clearly and make decisions.

"Ultimately, God allowed you to be — allowed it to happen," Ron explained to Twila. "We don't understand it. We may never understand it this side of heaven but we know we can trust God."

"Our promise, Hon," Emily added, "is one you've known since you were an itsy bitsy girl. 'And we know that in all things God works for the good of those who love him, who have been called according to his purpose.'"

Every day the three of them prayed together and thanked God for what had happened, for what He would do in their lives and for the couple who would be the baby's parents. Daily they claimed God's promise to make "all things work together for good," because they loved Him.

Although Twila could not remember meeting the Seaborns, she looked forward to living with them. It was decided she'd move down the first of September, in time for school to start. Their next biggest concern was for the baby.

"Can't Dawn and David take him?" From the beginning she refered to the baby as "he."

Emily felt the heavy responsibility of guiding her daughter. With every tough question Twila posed, Emily prayed the same prayer. *God, I know Your direction for Twila will be channeled through me. Keep me calm and level-headed.*

"I have no doubt they would like to take your baby, Twila, but there are a lot of things you will need to consider." Emily explained the problems they'd most likely run into in the future if such an arrangement were made. Twila understood the possible consequences and decided that giving her baby to her sister would not be the best solution for everyone involved.

"Your father and I love him, Twila, but it would be selfish if we keep him to satisfy our own emotional desires. I can't be a mother to you and him too. We're his grandparents and, to be perfectly honest, I've yet to see a child raised by a grandparent that turns out right. God never intended grandparents to be parents of their grandchildren. We have to do what is best for him."

"What if I choose to keep him?"

"We'll stand behind you, whatever choice you make, but you must understand you will be a single parent and like most single parents, you will have to give up a lot of things you would normally be doing at your age because he will be your responsibility until he is fully grown and on his own. We'll help you as much as we can."

"But I don't want to put him in a children's home."

"If he's adopted, Twila, he doesn't have to be in a children's home."

"Not even at first, until he's adopted?"

"Why no, Sweetheart. He'll be taken from the hospital and given to his parents the very same day. There are hundreds of young, Christian couples who can't have their own children, who are praying and waiting for a child. You can specify exactly what kind of home you want for him and he can have the immediate love of both a mother and a father."

Twila decided to place her child for adoption and prayed even more specifically for her baby's parents. She also began thinking about the requirements she wanted for his parents. "Mom, first of all, I want to be certain they're Christians."

"Does it matter to you what kind of church they go to?"

"Well, yeah, but can I say that, too?"

"I don't know why not."

"Hey, cool. I'll ask that they be Southern Baptist because when he's old enough, he'll be studying the same Bible lesson we do every week and every week we'll know what he's learning." Twila's face beamed at the thought.

ergeant Wood's chair squeaked as he shifted his weight and scooted closer to Twila. He was big, over six feet standing, but now he leaned forward on his chair, elbows on his knees and looked up into her frightened face. His red curls were stringy. Twila could smell his body sweat and feel the heat of his breath. He loomed like a living mountain before her.

Twila told what she could remember, totally embarrassed in spite of her effort to be as discrete as possible. She was surprised when she had to repeat her story and humiliated by Sergeant Wood's blunt, repetitive questions. She felt as if the walls were closing in on her.

"Your story's too vague," he accused, sticking his face into hers. "You're lying. Have you ever had sex before?"

"No."

"Did you know the guy?"

"No."

"How did he get into the house?"

"I guess through the patio door on the lower level."

"What were you wearing?" The sergeant scooted his chair closer.

"Shorts and a tee shirt." Twila pushed herself back into the chair. *He's got a Barney Fife mentality.*

"What kind of underwear did he have on?"

"I don't know."

"What color were his eyes?"

"I don't know."

A female officer sat off to the side. Twila recognized her from church. "Skiles," her name tag said, but Twila didn't really know much about her except that her son had committed suicide a year or so before.

"Now, Twila, we all sin," Officer Skiles said. "My son did when he killed himself, but he was a Christian and he's still going to heaven. You know, Twila, if you'll just tell us, let us know now, we'll talk to your parents about it. But see, if we find out later you're lying, you could end up in jail on a felony charge."

Twila glanced at her watch. Both her parents had assured her the police would listen to her story and ask a few questions and the whole report would be over in about an hour. Nearly two hours had passed. Wood accused her of lying and Skiles tried to get her to confess to sinning. They believed the pregnancy was her fault. She felt trapped.

What was all this talk about sin? Twila knew what sin was. She also knew that the police were trying to identify with her beliefs in order to get a confession. *What a ruse.*

"Well it says in the Bible all your sins will be found out, ya know? We all make mistakes and God forgives us of our sins," Officer Skiles persisted.

This isn't a mistake, nor have I sinned! Twila hated being patronized. She swallowed her anger knowing full well if she said more than the basic facts she'd be defensive and unkind. Using all the self-control she could muster, she calmly reminded herself, *I did not get myself pregnant. I was raped. If I lose my temper they'll never believe me and Mom will kill me.* She breathed deeply while huge tears of frustration rolled down her cheeks.

"Now tell me everything." Wood had his face in her's again. "What did you do?"

"I tried to get past him and he grabbed me by the arm. I couldn't get away."

"What then?"

"He hit me across the chest and knocked me down on the bed."

"Then what happened?" Not bothering to be genteel or tactful, Wood became crude, graphic. By the time the interrogation finally ended, Twila had endured a different kind of rape and again what should have been personal was insensitively exploited. The officers stripped from her the few remaining shreds of innocence and blasted away at her with accusing questions aimed to produce guilt.

"Why didn't you tell someone sooner? Why didn't you tell your parents? Why didn't you make a police report?"

Once allowed to leave the cluttered dirty office, Twila bore more guilt then she had ever known before. "They don't believe me. They think I'm lying," she cried bitterly as she clung to her mother.

"My daughter doesn't lie," Emily boldly stated when the officers walked up to them.

"Don't you think it's strange she talked to someone besides you?"

"Look, I'm thankful that my daughter has been trained to go to someone else. And think of who she went to, her Sunday school teacher and the youth pastor who is also her brother-in-law. What more could I ask? I'm grateful."

"Why didn't she report this sooner?"

"We didn't know until August 2 and we didn't report it sooner because we didn't want the church people to know yet. We didn't want it in the paper."

"Incidents of this nature involving juveniles are not reported to the press," Wood replied indifferently. "Now before you leave, we'd like her to look at some photos downstairs."

Emily went with Twila and watched as she flipped through the mug shots. The officers stood by talking between themselves.

"You know, I think there was a rape not long ago similar to this over in your same neighborhood." Wood looked at Emily. "Let me check the computer." He returned in minutes. "M.O., everything's the same."

For an hour Twila looked at faces, none of which matched the likeness in her mind.

"Do you have a school yearbook?" Wood asked. Twila nodded. "Dig it out and study every face in it. Here's my card," he said, handing her one. "I want you to call me if any picture reminds you of the guy you claim raped you. Give me the page number and name. Understand?"

"Yes, sir," Twila answered, placing his card in her purse. That Friday evening at home Twila looked through her school year books and she found a vaguely familiar picture. As directed, she called the police station and left the name under the picture and the page number.

Before they anticipated, gossip already circulating filtered back to Ron. The church leader had not only broken confidence, he let it be known he didn't believe Ron's story. Deeply hurt, Ron, Emily and Twila decided to share the truth publicly. Before the Sunday evening service, Ron met with his deacon board — with Emily present — and briefly told them of Twila's rape and consequent pregnancy. After the evening service he, with both Emily and Twila present, informed the entire youth department.

"Twila will be leaving Wednesday morning to stay with some friends of ours in Ft. Worth, Texas. We're telling you so you will know the truth." A wave of shock spread throughout the room. Twila's friends cried silently while cold looks of doubt passed between others.

Twila had just finished dressing when Emily answered the doorbell Monday morning and found Sergeant Wood and another officer at the door. "May we take a look through your house?" he asked.

"Why certainly," Emily said, and led them downstairs into what had been Twila's room.

"This just doesn't add up," Sargeant Wood said before going into the family room and out into the yard. When he came back into the house he said to Emily, "I don't understand how this could have happened."

"Well, it happened right after she became friends with Jeff."

"Who's Jeff?"

"Jeff Hanson. His father's an attorney in town. Twila met him on the school swim team but they're just friends. He graduated this year and he's in college now, I believe."

"Any other boyfriends?"

"No, not really. She had an interest in Steve James for awhile before the rape. They've been friends since we moved to Ft. Smith."

Wood asked for Steve's phone number and address and as he wrote them down, Twila explained, "We sort of saw each other a few times, that's all. He had a steady girlfriend when all this happened. He's been over since but we haven't dated or anything."

"Sergeant Wood," Emily interjected, "You need to understand, our girls haven't been permitted to go out on what generally is referred to as a date until they were sixteen, so Twila wasn't even dating when she became pregnant."

In the afternoon, Sergeant Wood was back again. "Twila, I've been to the school and talked to your friend, Steve, and I've been to the crisis pregnancy center. You lied to me about knowing whether or not you were pregnant. You told me you didn't know for sure that you were pregnant."

"I didn't." Twila felt more confident in her home territory. "I didn't know until I took a home test at my sister's in August."

"I can't imagine how it could have happened." Wood looked at Emily, shaking his head as if he pitied her naivete, while he left by the front walk. He stopped and turned back. "Why didn't she just go to the hospital the night it happened and get a shot of morning-after hormones? You wouldn't have to be worrying about all this."

Emily had never heard of a "morning-after shot" but she did recognize the sergeant's attitude.

"Mom," Twila said after the officer left, "If Sergeant Wood talked to Steve the way he did to me, Steve will never get over it. He's too shy and sensitive."

Ron leaned back in his tall, leather chair and stretched the weariness from his body. Every few days another wave of despair washed over him. Hearing of Twila's police interrogation on Friday, and the Sergeant's remarks to Emily earlier in the day, broke his heart. He knew Twila didn't want to file a report and although he hadn't demanded it of her, he did strongly encourage her to. "There's no other way the man can be stopped, Twila, unless women like yourself are willing to file police reports."

Ron naively assumed a sympathetic woman officer would discretely question Twila about the details and was shocked when the opposite occurred. Unable to concentrate on his work, Ron picked up a pencil and opened his journal.

Now we understand why many women refuse to go to the police and make reports of a rape. It was perhaps the most difficult day for Twila other than the day of the rape itself and the day she had to tell us … Why would a male officer be the one to interview a female rape victim? Why must they be so hard and caustic in their questioning?

It's almost time to take Twila to her new home in Texas ... It becomes heavier knowing our daughter will be moving out of her room ... not here ... to kiss goodnight ... not be here in the mornings to wake up and get off to school ... not here in the car with me on Sunday mornings, hair in curlers and all ... with her cheerful spirit, her smile and her terrific ability to have a lot of fun. How can we do without that in our lives?

Our daughter's courage has been a constant source of strength. Her willingness to go to the counselors we suggested, her desire to make a full police report in spite of the embarrassment, her desire to share it with all of her friends as a group before she left. ... Her willingness to go to a public school in another city.

Friendship has taken on new meaning ... You really do have only a very few genuine friends, those with whom you can trust the deepest feelings of your innermost being. To have friends to cry with you, call, write, send gifts, and make themselves available is an unbelievable comfort. Just to have someone there touching you, praying for you ...

God's promises are really true. The powerful passages that I've used hundreds of times to comfort others ... have indeed become living words to our spirit ...

Ron wrote out several familiar passages as he leafed through his Bible.

Trust in the Lord with all your heart ... and He shall direct your paths ... When you lie down you will not be afraid; ... For the Lord will be your confidence, and will keep your foot from being caught ... I will bless the Lord at all times; let us exalt His name together. I sought the Lord and He heard me, and delivered me from all my fears ... This poor man cried out and the Lord heard him. ... Do not fret because of evildoers ... for they heard Him ... for they shall soon be cut down like

the grass … Rest in the Lord and wait patiently
for Him; … I have been young and now I am old;
Yet I have not seen the righteous forsaken …
For the Lord loves justice and does not forsake
His saints; … But the descendants of the wicked
shall be cut off … God is our refuge and
strength … For so He gives His beloved sleep.

Tuesday afternoon, Thelma Bradford stopped by the Herrods' home.

"You're just on my mind so much, Emily, I know you're leaving tomorrow and you're right in the middle of packing for Twila."

"Oh, I'm doing fine." Emily appreciated Thelma's concern and she stopped from her packing long enough to give Thelma a warm hug. "You know how it is, until you stop, you don't think about it. It's when you stop that you think, so you don't stop until you have to." She laughed easily and shrugged her shoulders.

"Emily, I'd be so pleased if you'd let me help you drive to Ft. Worth tomorrow. In fact, Calvin said this morning, 'Honey, you must go with Emily.' And our daughter's down there now, remember? Besides, I'll get to see my grandsons."

Thelma arrived near noon on Wednesday as Emily and Twila finished loading the car. Ron had delayed going to the church office in order to see them off. "Emily," Thelma said, handing her an envelope, "Calvin asked me to give this to you. He woke up last night and felt the Lord impressed him to do this. It's to help out with your additional expenses."

As Thelma tucked her small bag in the car with Twila's Teddy bears and other necessities, Emily opened the envelope and pulled out a check.

"Honey. Look at this." Emily handed the check to Ron and turned to Thelma. "I'm so thankful. It's about what I've figured we'd need for maternity clothes and such for Twila. I decided right away I wanted her to look as nice as possible while she's pregnant."

September — December 1989

J eanne Seaborn was holding the back door open when Emily and Twila pulled into the driveway. "I see you've made it all right."

"Yes. I tell you, Jeanne, it was the biggest relief to hit Interstate 820 and have our headlights flash across the 'Welcome to Ft. Worth' sign. It's as if we'd finished a painful chapter of our lives."

"We're so glad you're here." Jeanne opened her arms and gave Emily and Twila welcoming hugs. "You must be worn out."

"Well, not too bad. Twila slept nearly the whole way in the back seat and a friend of ours came along to help drive." Emily explained about Thelma staying with her family as they carried their belongings into the house.

When Emily and Jeanne sat down, Twila kept standing, wide awake and bouncing with excitement. "Can I go see my room?" She knew the Seaborns had redecorated a room just for her.

"Of course you can." Jeanne laughed. "Just go down the hall there and see if you can find it. It has a double bed in it."

Twila came bounding back a minute later. "I know which one is mine." She was wearing a huge smile as she kicked off her tennis shoes.

"Well, you might be wrong," Emily warned gently.

"Oh, I can tell." Twila nodded her head enthusiastically. "Mother, it's got a neat tulip bedspread in blue and green — my favorite colors — and the walls are lemon white, puff maroon valances and white mini-blinds. It's so cool. Ms. Jeanne, I love the white furniture and Mother, you've got to see her big Snoopy and Peanuts ceramic dolls." Twila carried her Teddy bears in before her suitcases then joined the women in the kitchen for something to drink.

They talked about the pregnancy center, different adoption agencies and the doctor. Jeanne had already made appointments for the next day. Twila asked about the school, openly excited about the new experience. Once her questions were satisfied, she became very quiet. A pensive look flashed across her face.

"Mother, at my wedding can I still wear a white dress?" They both looked at Jeanne.

"Of course you will, Twila. Purity is different from virginity. Purity is an attitude of your mind."

"Sweetheart, you're going to have the whitest wedding dress we can find," Emily promised. "Jeanne is right. You're still pure, Twila because your heart is pure. You didn't do that act and you are just as pure in your heart and spirit as you ever were before this happened."

Twila sighed deeply and smiled her relief, then she hurried off to unpack.

"The extra bedroom," Jeanne explained later, "is reserved for you, Emily. Twila's welcome to sleep with you there in the extra twin bed or her own room, where ever she feels most comfortable."

Thursday night Emily wrote in her journal:

Our day to meet Fran Johnson at the Crisis Pregnancy center. She was all I knew she would be. Warm, sympathetic, understanding … as if we had known her for years. She was a tremendous help. Linda Sommers from Hope Agency was the same way.

I had such a peace today. It was as if I had finally found someone who knew the direction out of this terrible, complicated maze. My body is weak but my spirit is lifted.

Twila decided to sleep in the twin bed in Emily's room as long as Emily stayed. She enjoyed the security and closeness of her mother's company. "I really am glad to be out of Ft. Smith," Twila admitted to her mother. "Course I miss both Amys. I hope they can come down sometime. I wonder what school will be like here? I wonder if the kids are more like the ones in Kenner or Ft. Smith?"

Twila rambled on about school, how nice the ladies at the Crisis Pregnancy Center were and if there were any cute guys at church, until Emily's comments became sleepy grunts. Finally she said, "Twila, we've got to get to sleep. Your doctor's appointment's at 9:30 in the morning, and we've got to get you registered tomorrow afternoon and open a checking account. Besides, I've only heard half of what you've said the last ten minutes. I keep falling asleep."

"Will he do anything that hurts?"

"I don't know, Sweetie."

"What's he like?"

"All I know is his name's Dr. Benjamin McWilliams and he has two teenage daughters. Everybody says he's really nice."

"I still hate doctors." Twila expounded on her aversion while Emily drifted off to sleep.

In his journal dated Sunday, September 3, Dr. Herrod summarized his day.

```
      Twila always went to church with me early
on Sunday even though she was far from being
ready for church. She was there beside me in
the car, curlers in her hair, nothing quite
put all together yet and we prayed on the way
... Today I cried and prayed alone. It was a
good thing that Bailey Smith was preaching
today and not Ron Herrod. Surely this would
be the hardest time.
```

Monday, Ron flew in for a Labor Day picnic with the entire Seaborn family, four married children, their spouses and seven grandchildren.

The Seaborns' two adult sons quickly melted any inhibitions Twila might have felt as she flitted around in the middle of all the action. Her ability to laugh at herself made her a perfect target for Neil Seaborn's finely honed sense of humor.

"Look at all that food," he taunted when she filled her plate. "Must be eating for triplets."

"At least I have a reason for my indulgences," Twila fired back with a huge grin splitting her face. "What's yours?"

"Seriously, Twila," Neil said, his thoughts masked by false sobriety. "I've been giving a good deal of thought to your baby's name." Neil raised his voice over the din of the table chatter. "Even talked it over with Dad."

Miles picked up the signal from across the table. "He certainly did."

Twila didn't miss the looks exchanged between Miles and his son Neil before Miles asked for someone to pass the chips.

"We've decided," Neil continued, "That since you've become a part of our family you really ought to name your baby after someone in our family."

"Absolutely," Miles agreed without missing a beat. "We couldn't decide whether it should be 'Sadie' after my mother or 'Maude' after Jeanne's."

"Yuck." Twila wrinkled her nose in disgust. "And what if it's a boy?"

"No problem." Neil stood and clapped his hands. "Everybody, Twila's just given us permission to name her baby if it's a boy. The floor is now open for suggestions ..."

"I'm so glad you could make it down," Emily said when she and Ron had a few moments together. "The reality of everything hit home again Thursday morning when I started checking the boxes on the patient form at Dr. McWilliams' office. Single. Sixteen. Pregnant. It was just like, ugh, I hadn't even met those people and there I was telling them my daughter was pregnant."

"I'm glad it was you and not me." Ron smiled teasingly. "After all, you left me at Ft. Smith with everything there."

"I'd rather take care of things here than be there, that's for sure," Emily admitted, "but I do feel as if we're neglecting Dawn and Joey."

David and Dawn had made one trip to Florida in view of a call to a different church, so their lives were unsettled. Joey had recently found himself alone after a long-standing relationship.

That evening, Emily expressed more of her feelings by writing in her journal:

> Twila in her youth and innocence is not, or does not seem to be, any way affected by this. It's just another move in her life.
>
> However, as her mother, I feel the full load. Knowing that every decision I make, every direction I point Twila in, every word I say, every expression, attitude, reaction — all is vitally important for Twila's life now and the future.
>
> Even though it had been another day when my emotions have been overwhelmed, I must and will keep a positive and encouraging attitude for my precious baby, Twila.

What would you like to do this weekend, JoAnn?" John had been on the phone talking to some of his friends but looked rather deflated as he sank down on the couch beside his wife.

"I thought you were going to go golfing with some of the guys?"

"So did I, but they all seem to be taking Labor Day weekend to spend time with their families. If they're not shopping for school clothes, they're off on the last family picnic of the summer."

JoAnn had experienced the same "left out" feeling. Although they had honestly shared their frustrations, neither allowed themselves to be paralyzed by them.

"Let's go look at rocking chairs so we'll know what we want when the time comes."

"But you have one."

"The little one in the nursery? It's fine for a little rocking now and then, but it will never do if one of us has to be up half the night with a baby. We need to find one with a high back that is comfortable enough to sleep in."

"Guess that makes sense." John stood and offered his arm. "Let's go. Then we'll have dinner at Trotter's afterwards. I'm in the mood for ribs."

On Wednesday morning, Ron and Emily dropped Twila off at her new school, and then headed home to Ft. Smith. The next morning, Ron headed down the stairs to his office, coffee cup in hand. Just walking by Twila's empty bedroom tore at his heart. Passing through the family room to his office, the now familiar cold wave of failure washed over him.

Ron paused at his bookcase and looked at their family picture. Dawn was married, in her own home. Joey was away in graduate school. With Twila gone the house felt so empty — prematurely empty.

Ron sat at his desk and opened his Bible. Every day for the past month he'd taken comfort in the familiar words of Psalm 34: "I will bless the Lord at all times ... I sought the Lord, and He answered me, and delivered me from all my fears ... The eyes of the Lord are toward the righteous, and

His ears are open to their cry ... The Lord redeems the soul of His servants; and none of those who take refuge in Him will be condemned."

He had several letters to answer, but he pushed them aside, pulled a blue piece of stationery from his desk and started writing:

Sept. 4, 1989
My Dearest Twila,

As I begin to write this, I realize I haven't written you enough letters during your 16 years — forgive me ... I really want to be the best dad for you.

Since Aug 1, it has been the most difficult month of my life. I realize that you have been under awesome pressure for more than four months and your mom and I hurt for you.

Missing you at church Sunday, coming home to an empty house and letting you off at a strange school has been very hard for me ...

I love you so deeply.

I pray for you constantly.

I am so proud of you for ... the way you have handled this ...

The love and trust you have shared ...

Your mature decision to make unselfish plans for your baby to have a life that is best for the baby and for the parents. They are so blessed to receive a child that will probably be like you. I am also very proud of your life for the Lord!

There will be many dark times for you but there are several things you can count on —

Your mom and dad's love for you.

Jesus will never fail you.

The Word of God will strengthen you when you are weak.

The Church is still the best support group available.

God always has some special people like the Seaborns just when you need them.

He has something very special for you. I can't wait to see what the future holds.

With Unconditional Love - Dad

Ron and Emily sensed each other's inconsolable grief. Each felt the need to wrestle with thoughts of the future. They both thought of Job. Emily knew she and Ron had feared God and shunned evil all their lives. She identified with the hedge of protection that God had placed around Job. She'd always known that protection. Until now, God had never allowed that hedge to be broken.

"All things work together for good ..." How could this be good? Ron wondered. Still, in his heart he made the same vow to God as Job, *"Though He slay me, still will I trust Him."*

Emily began weekly trips to Ft. Worth, leaving Friday morning to arrive in time to meet Twila after school. Often she'd help Twila review her studies. Saturdays they spent shopping the malls and Sundays they attended church with the Seaborns.

During the week, Twila called home every night. "Hi, Mom. What's going on?"

"Nothing, just the usual."

"Hi, Knothead." Ron greeted over the extension. "How was your day?"

"Great, Dad. Ms. Jeanne let me drive her car today. I mean, she was going someplace so she let me drive. I've got everything down pat but parallel parking."

"Maybe Mother can work with you on that Saturday when she comes down."

"How are you feeling, Twila?"

"My back aches and I get these funny pains in my stomach. I've gotten some funny red lines on my stomach and they sting and itch."

"Sounds like stretch marks, Sweetie, and that's normal. It's not uncommon to have some aches and pains," Emily comforted.

Ron and Emily let Twila talk as long as she wanted every night, giving her whatever encouragement they sensed she needed. Their own feelings they kept to themselves. Although Emily no longer found time to write in her journal, Ron found it a place to clarify his feelings:

```
     Twila  calls  and  there  are  pains  and
discomforts  that  she  can't  understand.  No
sixteen  year  old  should  have  to  understand
these   kinds   of   pains   and   physical
complications  but  this  is  my  baby  having  a
baby  and  that's  hard  for  me  to  understand.
     Lord,  I  pray  that  you  will  use  this  time
that  is  so  difficult  to  develop  Twila  into  a
godly  woman  whose  life  will  bring  great  glory
to  Your  Name.
```

Kaay often talked with Emily about women's meetings at church, and she always asked about Twila. Never had she heard Emily sound so discouraged.

Paul and Calvin, both deacons, saw Ron more frequently, and although his sermons reflected his deeper walk with the Lord, they saw the sparkle leave his eyes and the spring leave his step. They agreed to visit the Herrods together just to express their love and offer support.

The Herrods' phone rang. For once in her life, Emily wished the caller was a salesperson so she wouldn't have to talk to anyone she knew.

"Emily, this is Kaay. Paul and Calvin ran into each other today and asked me to call you. The four of us would like to stop by for a little while tonight. Would that be convenient?"

"Oh my," Emily sighed heavily. "I don't know. We're neither of us going to be much company, I'm afraid."

"Well, you don't have to worry about us being company. We won't stay long so don't worry about fixing coffee or anything. Will seven thirty be all right?"

"Yeah, I guess so," Emily agreed reluctantly.

After the two couples left, Emily confessed to Ron, "I really didn't want to see anyone. But I have to admit I feel better since they came."

"It's marvelous how they've stood by us so faithfully." Ron agreed as he rinsed out a cup at the sink.

David and Dawn accepted a call to Trinity Baptist Church in Oscala, Florida but before they left in November they planned a weekend in Ft. Worth to visit Twila. Their plans grew to include two carloads of girls from Twila's Sunday school class. Carolyn Plummer drove the second car.

Carolyn sat with David, Dawn and Jeanne at the kitchen table, visiting and watching the girls in the family room. Three of the girls with boyfriends sat on the couch dreaming their way through the pages of *Modern Bride* and another five girls in various postures each held a hand on Twila's stomach. She laid on her back in the middle of the floor.

"He always kicks this time of night."

"Doesn't it feel weird?" Alice, Carolyn's daughter was a couple of years younger but was accepted as part of the group.

"Feels like he's doing gymnastics," she giggled. "Hurry, he's kicking again."

Modern Bride hit the floor along with the coffee table that tipped as the trio all scrambled to find a place on Twila's stomach for their hands.

"Cool." The favorite expression passed everyone's lips as they waited, holding their breaths in unison as they waited to feel another flutter of life.

"It's this bitterness, Kaay," Emily confided. "Every Monday I drop Twila off at school — she's showing more all the time and she's so vulnerable. I hate whoever did it. And Christians we thought were our friends believe it is her fault. I get so angry. I just can't give it up. I've tried and I've tried and I think I've forgiven them, but it keeps coming back."

"Emily, keep giving it up," Kaay encouraged, not asking for more details. "Keep doing whatever you're doing and I'm sure the victory will come."

O f course Emily's bitterness keeeeps coming back. Every time she sees her precioussss baby, I remind her.

I remind her of allll she's lost. Allll Twila has lost. I remind her of every possssible complication that could develop with the pregnancy. I remind her that her firssst grandchild is of ignoble birth. I remind her of the people she thought were friends.

Most of all I remind her of how the family's reputation has been besmirched. Their precious reputation. Gone — and all their influence with it.

The Life Action crusade started October 19, and on the last Thursday, October 21, the topic was bitterness. Ron and Emily knew the familiar words the speaker read. "Let all bitterness, wrath, anger ... be put away from you with all malice: And be ye kind one to another ... forgiving ... as God for Christ's sake has forgiven you."

Ron and Emily both recognized their growing bitterness toward the rapist, their church, the town and what their bitterness was doing to them. When the invitation was given at the close of the service, they were among the first to slip from their seats and make their way back to the prayer room.

At first, they just talked. "Ron, every time I'm out, I'm looking for that person. I could still kill him."

"I know, I feel the same way. And since the rape, the rumors that have come back through the Ft. Smith political grapevine ..." He shook his head and shrugged helplessly. "Everything I do is suspect. I'm bitter, too."

With no more feeling than they had months before when they obediently thanked God for Twila's rape and subsequent pregnancy, Ron and Emily knelt together and confessed their bitterness to God. First one and then the other prayed, "Lord, I am bitter, forgive me." As they confessed their resentment, their bitterness drained and their hearts were filled with love.

When they left the prayer room Officer Harry Stevens, from ballistics, came up to them. "How did Twila describe this man?" he asked. One question led to another and he finally said, "Thought you'd like to know we arrested a suspect today, actually booked him on burglary."

"Burglary?" Ron asked.

"I don't have all the details but he was picked up on possession of stolen property and illegal firearms. The rifle was traced back to his neighbor, a woman who'd filed a rape report about a month after Twila. Why don't you call up in the morning and ask for the detective on the case and see what he knows about Twila?"

"Criminal detective, please." Ron's first phone call Friday morning was to the police station.

"One moment sir, and I'll transfer your call." The wait was brief.

"Detective Moore, may I help you?"

"I understand you apprehended a suspected rapist yesterday and I'd like to know if you are familiar with my daughter's rape?"

"I haven't gotten any reports on it. Was there a report made?"

"Yes, near the end of August. Sergeant Wood did the interrogation. I understand he indicated he didn't believe her story but there's no doubt about it in our minds."

"I wonder where the report is?"

"I believe it's right there in your computer. We have a copy of it."

"Give me a few minutes to pull it up and I'll get back with you." Moore called back in less than an hour. "I've got the report. Do you live next to the Marrow residence?"

"Well, I don't know all of my neighbors. We're at 5900 Cliff Drive."

"How soon can I come out and talk to you?" He came immediately.

File in hand, Detective Moore walked through the family room, into Twila's bedroom and out the patio door and then stood, staring at the report and shaking his head. "Where has this been?"

"In your computer the whole time," Ron replied, as confounded as the detective.

For over two hours Moore kept looking around and re-reading the report. Ron had to leave and Emily followed the detective as he continued his investigation. "Sergeant Wood said there were problems with her story. He told me

Twila lied." Detective Moore kept shaking his head in unbelief as Emily repeated Twila's story.

The following week, Emily went to Ron's study door. "I didn't get his name, but it's the district attorney on the phone."

Later Ron relayed the conversation to Emily. "The detective has turned everything over to the D.A. He said the picture Twila picked out of the yearbook is of the suspect they are holding, and it sounds like this guy, Eugene, raped our neighbor directly behind us, too."

"So he's raped two?"

"Possibly more. One woman submitted to DNA testing at the time of her rape and plans to press charges. It's about the only way to get a conviction."

Emily arrived home on November 6 in time to say goodbye to David and Dawn before they left for Florida. "I only wish I could have been home to help you pack. We've had so little time together lately."

"We understand, Mother," Dawn assured her. "When it's all over, you can come down for a visit."

Visit the rapist. Ron recognized God's prompting. He had heard His voice when he entered the ministry, when he left one church and took another. He felt it when he was impressed to preach on certain topics or to visit individuals in need. But to visit a possible rapist? The man who the police believed ravished his own little girl?

Visit the rapist in jail? What would I say? For months Ron had had much to say. The bitterness he felt went beyond mere words — but all that was gone.

"I'd like to see Eugene Marrow, please." Deputies at the Ft. Smith jail recognized Ron as pastor of the First Baptist Church and nodded for Ron to follow. His footsteps blended with the echo of the deputy's in the empty corridors as they made their way to the holding cell. The clang and rattle of the cell door opening was as chilling as the feel of the cold metal bars.

"It will be just a few minutes, sir," the officer stated. "And let me forewarn you. Some inmates roughed him up pretty good so the kid's really bruised up." Surprise creased Ron's brow so the officer explained. "Murderers have more respect from fellow inmates then rapists."

Ron sat alone with his thoughts. *Murderers have more respect than rapists? They've beaten him up? That's ridiculous. They all deserve — but so do I. I wanted to kill. I could have killed. I deserve death, too.* Ron knew God's forgiveness. His head dropped as a new understanding of humility swept over him. Compassion, like sweetened yeast, began to swell in his heart toward the man he'd come to see.

Ron heard footsteps. His heart skipped a beat and started racing. *What will I feel when I actually see him? Will the hatred come back? After all, he stole my baby's innocence, he raped — I wanted to murder. He's a criminal — me, prominent pastor of the large First Baptist Church — we're the same without God's forgiveness.* An urgency to witness to the young man gripped Ron's heart. *God, can this man's life be salvaged?*

Ron looked up. *He's younger than Joey.* Pity knotted Ron's stomach as the barred door clanged shut. The lock clicked. Finally, Ron stood facing the man his girl had identified as her rapist. He waited for the angry feelings that never came. Instead, Ron felt an odd mix of pity and urgency to reach out to the young man whose sunken grey eyes passed suspiciously over him. He noted Eugene's lacerated skin looked sallow against the orange of his wrinkled jumpsuit.

"I'm the pastor from the First Baptist Church," Ron said, extending his hand. Eugene's hand was cold and limp in Ron's grip. No sign of recognition altered the mask of indifference on Eugene's badly bruised face.

"I used to go to that church," Eugene said, and shrugged slightly. "When I was a kid." For a moment Ron hoped for a crack in the invisible barrier he felt between them.

"I understand you're having some difficulties and I wanted you to know I have a concern for you." Eugene offered no other comment as they sat down together on the single hard bench.

"Do you remember when you attended our church, what you were taught about being saved?" Eugene shrugged indifferently.

"Eugene, God says we're all sinners. He teaches us in the Bible that He sent His Son, Jesus, to take our punishment. He has forgiven us." Ron explained God's love again, sin, repentance and forgiveness, wanting to make sure Eugene understood. "Did you ever accept God's forgiveness and receive His gift of salvation?"

"I went forward when I was thirteen in one of your church camps. Mom changed churches a couple of years after that and I just stopped going."

"Eugene, are you sure you have received Christ and will go to heaven when you die?"

"Yeah."

Ron knew there was very little evidence of Eugene's salvation, but at this point he realized he couldn't argue with Eugene or press the issue.

"What about your father?"

"Alcoholic. Moved out when I was sixteen." Eugene spoke with his eyes staring straight ahead. Was there a slight catch in his voice when he spoke of his father? A difference maybe, in the tone of his voice? *Joey and I played golf and watched ball games together when he was sixteen. He went on revivals with me.*

"Would you object if I prayed with you?"

"If you want." After praying, Ron stood to go. He looked once more into Eugene's face, this time for any sign of remorse, any appeal for help. There was none.

"I've one other question, Eugene. Did anyone from our church ever come visit you?"

"No. Never did."

"God forgive me," Ron prayed later as he stood at his living room window and looked through trees at the roof of Eugene Marrow's home. *To think he lived less than a block away.*

J ohn, sensitive to JoAnn's pain of childlessness as another Christmas season approached, knew they both needed something to look forward to. "Let's go to Hawaii after Christmas," he suggested. "Maybe we can even stay in our honeymoon suite."

"Oh, John, could we?" Her excitement died quickly when she got to work the next day and another employee asked for a personal day off. "I'm having an abortion so Friday would be best," she explained. "It'll give me the weekend to recoup. I should be fine by Monday. I was the last time."

JoAnn talked with her old friend, Donna, that night on the phone. "I'd learn to be happy with two kids, just two and a dog, and a big house and a station wagon."

"You know, JoAnn, I have an older sister. She's beautiful, well educated, thirty and doesn't even have a husband yet. At least you have a husband who loves you."

At least you have a husband who loves you. It was like God had carved the words in JoAnn's mind. Gradually she began to look at her life realistically. Yes, she did have a husband. He was thoughtful and kind and always her best friend. They had fun together. They were happy.

JoAnn realized she had to deal with her ungrateful spirit.

"Mom, come quick. He's kicking." Emily jumped out of her bed and rushed to Twila. "Where my hand is. Here." Twila took her mother's hand, directing it to the right area of her bulging stomach. "Now wait, he's just getting warmed up." Emily could hear the smile in her daughter's voice. "I know, let's sing to him."

Emily kept her hand on Twila's stomach and wiggled around enough to make herself comfortable on the floor beside Twila's bed. In the semi-darkness of the bedroom they nodded and smiled to each other, aware of several kicks while they sang verses of *"Jesus Loves Me."* He kicked less as they sang *"Away In A Manger"* and by the time they finished *"Silent Night,"* his kicking stopped.

"At least this kid will know good music when he hears it." Twila laughed at her own humor, then her mind jumped to something else. "Does it hurt an awful lot, Mom, I mean when you're having a baby?"

"Yes, Twila but it's different. It's not constant. And Dr. McWilliams said he wouldn't let you have a long hard labor and I promise you, Sweetheart, I'm going to be right there with you the whole time. You're going to do just fine."

"Do you think he hears us talk and knows our voices?"

"We know babies hear. I'd suppose they're able to recognize familiar voices." Emily yawned.

"I'm glad we said we wanted his parents to be college educated. I wonder what they have degrees in?"

"Daddy sort of wanted his father to be in the ministry. Did you request non-smokers?"

"Of course. Hey, little fellow, maybe your daddy will be a preacher like your grandpa and you can grow up and love

Jesus and be a preacher, too." Emily fell asleep listening to Twila talk to her baby.

Nearly all flights from Ft. Smith made connections in the Dallas/Ft. Worth International Airport, so as often as he could Ron would spend a few hours or a night at the Seaborns to be with Twila. Between times, however, he filled in the gaps with letters. This he did, shortly before their Thanksgiving together in Mobile.

> My Dearest Twila,
>
> I hope this letter finds you feeling well and carrying on your busy schedule. I have never been prouder of you than I am now. Your grades and success with your driving are great steps forward. But most of all, the way you have handled your situation and the way you are growing and maturing, make me so very proud. You are a great young lady.
>
> I love you and miss you so much. Just think — in less than three months we will have you home, your baby will have two great parents and they will have America's best grandbaby!
>
> This has been a hurting time for all of us but we have learned so much and God is preparing us all for some very special things.
>
> I am praying special things for you — that you will remain physically strong and recover quickly after delivery, that you will remain joyful, that you will stay close to the Lord, that we will be able to minister for Jesus together in some way.
>
> Please pray for me to be able to know God's will — I am so anxious to see you at Thanksgiving. You are my girl, Knothead.
>
> Your Dad.

Ron and Emily arrived in Mobile for Thanksgiving before Twila's flight from Ft. Worth and told their parents of her situation. They had overcome the initial shock before Twila arrived and everyone endeavored to enjoy the brief holiday together.

After Thanksgiving, Twila began taking less of an active part in the church youth activities but she still had fun on Sunday and Wednesday nights. Cory, one of the guys in the youth group, was always fun to be around. One Sunday evening, he was in a particularly funny mood and bulged his stomach way out in front. "My stomach's as big as yours," he teased.

"Oh, yeah?" Twila hooked her fingers together under her stomach and turned sideways. "Anyone want to judge?" She stood beside Cory and had her good friend, Jennifer, snap a profile picture.

Although the guys were friendly and enjoyed her spontaneity, no one would date her. "I understand," she explained to Jennifer, "but I hate it."

During one of Ron's visits to Ft. Worth, Miles explained that Birchman Baptist Church supported a large number of missionaries and owned nearly a half dozen small homes to provide housing for the missionaries when they were in the States.

"We have a small house that's empty, Ron," Miles offered, "if you and Emily would like to have Christmas here together as a family." Miles arranged to give them the key and Ron planned for a few days off. Emily made lists of things to take and food to buy once they arrived. She took extra clothes because she'd be staying in Ft. Worth after Christmas until the baby arrived.

December 1989 — January 1990

Monday evening, December 18, Ron and Emily debated whether or not to leave Ft. Smith. A cold front had moved in, bringing freezing rain, but Twila expected them in Ft. Worth in the morning. They couldn't disappoint her.

It took over an hour to creep the two miles to the closest service station. "I think we'd better buy some de-icer," Ron explained as he pulled into the station. For the next sixty miles they were forced to stop frequently and spray the windshield.

At 5:00 a.m., they crawled into bed at the mission house. They slept only a few hours before going out to buy a tree. Emily was determined to have it trimmed before they picked up Twila from school that afternoon.

Joey completed his degree is Business Administration at the University of Arkansas, Fayetteville and accepted a position at Mercy Hospital in Oklahoma City. He moved to Oklahoma the weekend before Christmas, having only enough time to unload into his apartment before driving to Ft. Worth late Christmas Eve.

By nature, Joey looked at realities. Although sickened and angry when he learned Twila had been raped, he realized there was little he could do. He couldn't make a wrong into a right. He couldn't undo the pregnancy. He could only go on with his schooling and talk to her whenever possible and those times had been few.

Joey wasn't prepared for the unfamiliar, little house. The family was incomplete without Dawn and the usual hordes of people bouncing in and out, filling the house with Christmas joy. The isolation and quiet, empty hours, coupled with the artificial "home" environment made Joey feel imprisoned.

True, his mother had decorated the tree with memorable family ornaments. She had made their traditional seafood gumbo and had baked their usual Christmas cookies. She'd worked hard and he was grateful. Yet his dad was tense, which made Emily tense and that made the kids tense. Everything was off-key.

Joey knew that coupled with the stress of the church were all the consequences of the rape. Hidden beyond his parents' positive caring for Twila was the burden of heartbreak they endured. Joey marveled at Twila's ability to laugh and spar with him. Her infectious smile hadn't changed, but still, he couldn't ignore his kid sister's condition — her swollen hands and feet. It was all so unfair, especially her upcoming delivery and the foreboding thought of giving away the child who was a part of all of them.

The subdued quartet exchanged gifts without the usual carefree laughter and telephone interruptions. Joey appreciated his new clothes, and was slightly amused at his dad's nonplussed reaction over a telephone from Emily that was a replica of a mallard duck.

"Mother, I like this," Twila squealed as she held up a jumper Emily had made for her.

"It's something you can wear after the baby's born, Twee Dee. I made Dawn one, too."

Gee. Twila's so big and slow, Joey thought. *Funny how she's still the kid sister in my mind, the little brat who always wanted to be "in" with her big brother and sister.*

When Joey left the day after Christmas, he was angry at the man who'd stolen his little sister's childhood and robbed so much joy from his family, yet there was pity for him, too.

He'll never do what I'm doing — beginning a new exciting life in a new city and a new career. The guy's headed for prison with the cause of his problems unsolved and his life destroyed. He was a victim, too.

It had been eight years since John and JoAnn had honeymooned in Hawaii, but the sound of the breaking waves and the feel of warm sand between their toes felt the same.

"Hawaii has been even better than what I imagined. Too bad we don't have a couple more days." JoAnn fastened her seat belt, pulled a book out of her carry-on bag and settled back in the seat.

"It's been sorta neat, stirring up so many memories," John said as he snapped the overhead storage door shut and settled into the seat next to his wife. Before he buckled in, he pulled a book of tickets from his shirt pocket. "Here, Sweetheart, your extra two days."

"My what?"

"Just thought you'd like to stop by your folks for a couple of days before we head back home. Take in a day on the slopes, get a hug from your mother." John talked as casually as if they were going to buy a loaf of bread, and he loved every second of JoAnn's surprised reaction.

"But work? You're due back tomorrow."

"Yeah, well." John shrugged, took a deep breath and scratched his head. "Don't you suppose they can manage without me another couple of days?"

"But you can't just not show up."

"I sorta figured that, so I made a couple of phone calls."

"John!" JoAnn covered her mouth. Half laughing and half crying she sputtered, "I'd hug you but I'm buckled in and I don't want to crush the orchid you gave me."

"It's all right, Sweetie, you can hug me later." He ran a finger under the rim of her eye and caught a tear threatening to spill.

I t was late New Year's Day when Ron headed north on the freeway alone. The thought of leaving Emily behind for three weeks, with Twila so near her due date and returning to an empty house and the troubled church, drained the last reserves from his emotional barrel.

As he drove, Ron reflected on his ministry, the wonderful years of growth and expansion in Kenner, and now the discouraging spirit of the Ft. Smith church. In his visits with Miles over the holidays, Ron had been very open.

"I've always felt that with prayer and enough time, I could solve any problem, any situation, but I've come to understand some things just don't turn around and that's a fact of life. Still, I can't play their church games.

"Then there's my own personal struggle. To this day I wonder if I made a mistake in moving. If I'd stayed, would things have continued well at Kenner? Would my daughter have remained unharmed? Did I miss God's call, somehow?"

Like the white lines racing toward him, the questions repeated themselves over and over through the long, dark night. Fatigue crept through him, and gravel seemed to line his heavy eyelids, blurring his vision. Finally, at 2:00 a.m. he pulled up to the first stop sign in Ft. Smith, then another and another.

As his headlights caught his own driveway, red lights flashed in his rear view mirror. Ron pulled over and rolled his window down.

The officer approached, shining his flashlight into the back of the car. "May I see your driver's license, please?" Ron pulled his wallet from his back pocket and gave the officer his license.

"Have you been drinking? You were weaving quite a bit back there."

"No, sir. I don't drink but I am very sleepy. You see, I've just driven in from Ft. Worth and I'm dead tired, but if you'd be so kind as to let me pull into my driveway there I'll be off the road."

"You live here?"

"My home. Yes, sir."

The officer nodded curtly.

"Thank you, Officer." Ron's voice was hoarse with fatigue.

Ron's fumbled in the dark for the light switch, then headed to his downstairs office. He could smell the wetness even before his shoes sunk into the water-soaked carpet.

Twila's condition was too unjust, the separation from Emily too great, the distance too far, the church too discouraging — and broken water pipes too overwhelming. Ron turned off the main water valve and collapsed onto the couch. Feeling utterly helpless and totally dejected, he buried his head in his hands and wept.

How abysmally sublime! What's the matter, Dr. Herrod? Are you a bit short of jooooy tonight?

No sweeeet memories of a "blesssed" Christmas this year? Soooo alone. No beeeeautiful wife to console you. No sweeet little girl to make you smile.

How successful do you feel now, Ron? What about praying, now? How about some praaaaise?

If only his adoooring church members and deeear friends could see him now.

W hen Twila went in for her checkup after the New Year, Dr. McWilliams observed increased swelling. "I think it best for you to finish this semester at home," he advised. The following visit, he set Friday, January 19 to induce labor. "Emily," he explained, "With Twila's pre-toxic condition it's time she delivered. The baby's a good size. I also think that emotionally she needs to get past the pregnancy, get back to her home with you and her father and get on with her life."

"And if the labor becomes difficult?"

"I won't let it. Because Twila's small and her bone structure isn't fully developed, a cesarean section is a viable option. We'll watch her very closely."

"Does that mean I won't be able to be with her?" Emily asked anxiously. "I promised her I'd be with her through the whole thing."

Dr. McWilliams hesitated only a minute. "It'll be all right. You can still go in with her."

J oAnn picked up the phone and recognized Ted Watson's voice immediately. "Do you have a baby for us?" She could have bitten her tongue off for speaking so quickly.

"I only called to see if I could come over for a visit. It's been quite awhile. I'd just like to ask a few questions."

JoAnn set a time for the next afternoon, then called John at work. "I wanted to give you a chance to get off work to be here, if you could," she explained. John was home the next afternoon when Ted arrived.

"Do you still want a baby as much as you did?"

"Oh, by all means," John spoke without hesitancy.

"Are you prepared for a baby?"

"The nursery, the car seat, the crib, are all ready and waiting." JoAnn had a hard time not sounding impatient.

"Do you have any more plans for a vacation soon?"

"No, we just got back from Hawaii, you know, and John surprised me by adding a couple of days in Seattle. Do you have something pending?" By now, JoAnn fully expected to hear him say, "We may have" — but instead she got another vague promise.

"I hope sometime this year we'll be able to work with you."

John reached over and squeezed her hand.

When Ted left, JoAnn felt more discouraged than ever. She cried awhile and then called her mother.

D awn flew in from Florida and she, Emily and Twila went shopping. "Mom, I want my little guy to go to his parents looking loved and cared for," Twila said. They all agreed and went to the nicest baby shops around to find the perfect all-pink and all-blue baby outfits in Ft. Worth.

"Now, I want you to understand," Emily explained to the clerk, "one of these outfits will be coming back."

Ron and Emily checked Twila into All Saints Episcopal Hospital at 7:00 a.m. on January 19. Ron had been in hospitals hundreds of times, yet never got over feeling queasy. It was worse seeing his daughter hooked up to monitors and an I.V., so he occupied himself more out of Twila's room than in it. By mid-morning Dawn arrived and Ron settled into waiting in the cozy, yet fully equipped, birthing room

Dr. McWilliams stopped by at noon and confirmed that not only was Twila's mild labor unproductive but her blood pressure was elevated. She was relieved by the doctor's promise. "If you haven't done anything by 5:00, we'll go ahead with a C-section."

At 5:30 Emily found herself trying to help Twila through an uncomfortable epidural and at the same time listen to a technician explain how she was to don a scrub suit. As the epidural took effect, Emily was given her final instructions. "Wait down the hall by surgery and someone will get you when we're ready."

Emily found the corridor a typically impersonal, waxy yellow with nothing other than steel-grey surgery doors on which to focus her attention. She forced herself to pray rather than to think about the surgery she would soon witness. With no medical background or experience to prepare her for what she was about to face, and feeling totally alone, she cried out in her heart, "Oh Lord, You got me this far. I know You're going to get me the rest of the way."

In less then five minutes, Emily was sitting on a stool and holding Twila's free hand. A small twelve-inch-high screen stretched across Twila's chest and blocked her vision.

From where Emily sat she saw her daughter's face in the same view as the bright crimson line trailing the scalpel the doctor drew across Twila's taut abdomen. The amplified heartbeat of the unborn child marked the seconds of the empty silence.

"We're fixing to break the water," Dr. McWillaims explained, "once we do that, we have to work fast."

Emily translated his work into a comforting stream of words for Twila, even when the doctor's hand disappeared inside Twila's stomach.

"Okay, push," the doctor instructed his assistant.

Starting just below Twila's ribs, the assistant pushed downward and immediately Dr. McWilliams retrieved a perfect, wiggling form.

"It's a boy, Twila," and at that moment Emily's mind flashed back to the very first time she heard her grandson's heartbeat. Through her tears she smiled and said, "Sweetheart, they've already got a blanket around him and they're putting him in the bassinet."

Dr. McWilliams looked at Emily for the first time since he started the delivery. "Go over and see your grandson."

"Okay." Emily was a bit surprised. "Twila, can I go over and see?"

"Yeah." Twila's smile was a burst of sunshine. "Go see him and tell me if he's all right."

Emily stepped over to the nurse attending the baby. "I'd like to hold him," Emily's request was met with a begrudging stare.

"Let her hold him." Dr. McWilliams' voice was one the nurse could not ignore. Emily took her grandson and carried him over for Twila to see.

In the waiting room, Emily walked directly to Ron. "We have a grandson," she said, her smile immediately washed with tears. Ron remembered his prayers committing the child to God for special service and his request for a grandson. His prayer, half answered, overwhelmed him and he too, wept openly as he encircled Emily in his arms.

Ron and Emily needed time to share their relief and joy, and to draw from each other the strength they needed to love the grandson they would have so little time to enjoy.

Joey arrived Friday evening and marveled at the relaxed atmosphere. "Mom, give him to Joey."

"No, no, that's fine. I'd probably make him cry or something." Joey kept his hands stashed in his pockets.

"Oh, don't be silly," Emily chided, giving Joey no choice. "He won't break." Emily settled her grandson into Joey's rigid arms. "Isn't he precious? See how perfect his little head is?"

Joey studied his nameless nephew. *How can they do this? How can everyone hold him and kiss on him and fall in love with him knowing that in two days they won't see him again for twenty-one years and maybe not even then?* "Glad to see you arrived safe and sound, kid. Here, Auntie." Joey stepped over to Dawn and placed the warm sleeping bundle in her arms. "It's your turn now." *I can't let myself love you, kid. I know it isn't right to feel this way but I can't handle loosing someone I love again.*

Dawn slept at the hospital Friday night. Saturday the family drifted in and out, taking turns holding the baby, snapping pictures of each other and savoring their limited time together. That evening Ron headed back to Ft. Smith. Emily spent the night with Twila.

Only those closest to Dr. Herrod could see the added strain on his face as he stepped onto the podium on National Right to Life Sunday, January 21, two days after his grandson had been born.

"... Since that infamous Roe versus Wade decision was made in 1973, 25,000,000 living, developing, growing, yet unborn babies have been brutally murdered in America's abortion chambers ... Every day 4,000 die at the hands of doctors in this nation. A woman in America ... can have her unborn child put to death at any time ... even if she's already in labor. The most dangerous place in America is in the womb of a mother.

"The English language itself is inadequate to describe properly the magnitude of this problem ... What Hitler did to the Jews, will, in the future, seem like a Sunday afternoon picnic to what America has done to the unborn. Abortion is America's holocaust.

"... The Bible tells us when life begins. Job 33:4 says that the spirit of God has made me, and the breath of the Almighty gives me life. Genesis 2:7 says the Lord God formed man out of the dust of the ground and breathed into his nostrils the breath of life and man became a living being.

"Human life began when God shaped Adam into His own image and breathed into him the breath of life and this life has been transmitted from generation to generation in an unbroken chain that links Adam and Eve to every child conceived in their mother's womb.

"... The one [argument] we're hearing a lot about today is the woman should have the right to decide what happens with her body. I would say amen, and amen, and amen ... She has a right to her body, but she has no right to take the life of that body within her womb.

"There are those who say, what about rape and incest? Shouldn't a woman have the right to abort in such cases? I want to say to you that rape is an unspeakably terrible crime against the victim. You're listening to a preacher who has a right, more than most, to be angry at a rapist. But I'm more angry at pro-abortionists using the victims of rape as one of their big guns for keeping abortion alive in this country."

Then Ron's voice broke and he paused. When he gained control of his emotions he continued.

"Today I want to take personal privilege and applaud a very special young lady in my life who's had the courage to give birth to a child ...

"... Those of you who know the history of this democracy know there was a time in every city and village and crossroads pulpit when they were aflame with God, when preachers shaped the moral and ethical standards of this nation ... Those days are gone ... Most of the pulpits are silent because preachers are afraid of what somebody will think or that it might cost them their jobs ... Thank God there are still some preachers who will call sin by its name and sinners to repentance ... Our pro-life God has provided for you forgiveness of sin and eternal life in the Lord Jesus Christ."

Emily and Dawn were reluctant to leave Twila Sunday evening but all three of them were tired and needed rest. Twila had her son with her the entire day and her stomach was hurting. "You'll have to be off all medication for twenty-four hours prior to signing the adoption papers," Linda Sommers from the Hope Agency had explained. Twila fully understood the legal requirements. She knew, too, that she had to be alone for the night — another requirement — so the law would be satisfied that she had sufficient time alone to make an independent decision regarding the placement of her child for adoption.

After John left for work, JoAnn took a soda and a book to the living room. The phone interrupted her reading shortly after 8:00 a.m.

"Hello."

"JoAnn, this is Ted. A situation has occurred which might involve you and John. Where are you going to be today?"

"Do I need to stay home?"

"Not necessarily. Where's John?"

"He's at work."

"Do you want us to call you or John?"

"Call John, because it might be hard to get ahold of me." JoAnn's heart raced and her hands trembled. "Has there been a baby born?"

"I can't tell you."

"Can you tell me anything?"

"No. And I'd advise you not to tell anyone anything. Just start praying but don't say anything and don't get your hopes up."

JoAnn hung the phone up. "Don't tell anyone?" she said aloud. "I'm a talker! I've got to tell someone."

First she called John. "Ted called. There's a situation ... he might call you at work. I'm going to call Mom. Bye."

Immediately she dialed her mother. It was six a.m. in Seattle. "I'm waiting for a baby, Mom," she cried with excitement. "There's a situation that might involve us, so start praying. I gotta go. Bye."

JoAnn's dear friend, Donna, in Houston, was next on her list and she repeated the same, short message. JoAnn made herself stop calling after telling only two of her closest friends in church. Then she bustled around trying to find things to do as she waited for Ted to phone. It was mid-morning before the phone finally rang.

"Have you heard anything?" John asked.

"No, I haven't heard a thing."

"I have. We are to be at the agency at 4:30. We have a baby boy."

R on, Emily and Dawn arrived at the hospital in time to watch Twila give her son his morning feeding. Then they took turns holding him until Twila was ready to dress him for his trip to his new home.

"Now, listen, Son, I gave you a good start, all eight pounds and two ounces and twenty-one inches of you, so you drink your milk and eat your vegetables." Twila chattered away above his wee cries. Once she had him dressed, she snuggled him close. "There, there, now you're just fine. Sh-h-h." Once he was quieted she continued her lecture.

"Now, the most important thing is for you to obey your parents and grow up loving Jesus. And I want you to go to church every Sunday and maybe someday, when you're big, you'll be a preacher just like your Grandpa."

"Dawn, look how that blue outfit picks up the blue in his eyes."

"Now, Mom, they're too dark to tell," Dawn replied.

"Well, now, it's a little hard to tell for sure, but I think he's going to have blue eyes just like Twila's. You know, I think he's even got the Herrod face."

"Poor kid." Twila's smile belied her words. "Did you remember the raccoon babybottle?"

"Yes, Sweetie, it's in that big envelope Daddy has, along with letters we're sending."

Emily had just finished her last roll of film when Ted Watson and Linda Sommers arrived. Dawn stood unobtrusively to the side of Twila's bed and Ron and Emily guarded their feelings through the necessary explanations, then watched as Twila signed away her precious son.

"Ted, we do have one request," Ron said as he stepped over to Dawn and took his grandson for the last time. "If his parents don't object, could we be told what they name him?" Ted nodded his answer as Ron kissed his grandson good-bye and tenderly placed him into Emily's hungry arms.

"You precious, little thing. Your Gremmy loves you very much." She held her cheek close to his before relinquishing him to Twila. "Here, Twila, I'm going to have mascara and lipstick all over his pretty little face if I keep this up."

Twila hugged him one last time as she stepped over to Linda. "See, he's got my blonde hair and I think it's even a bit curly." She gave him one last peck on the cheek and gently drew her finger across his tight little fist. "You be a good little boy, Son, and obey your mommy and daddy."

*"And we know that in **all things** God works for the good of those who love him, who have been called according to his purpose."*

Romans 8:28 (NIV)

The Taylors arrived five minutes before the appointed time. JoAnn walked straight from the doorway to her infant son. The staff went to an outer office as John trailed JoAnn and the two stood, awestruck at the beautiful child before them.

JoAnn scooped her son gently into her arms. Turning her face up to John's she said, "His birth mother must have loved him a lot to have dressed him so beautifully."

"Let me hold him." John requested. JoAnn watched his face as it was transformed by the tenderness a father reserves for his son. "Wait a minute." JoAnn grabbed their camera for the first picture of father and son. "Now, my turn," she said, trading the camera for the baby. "I can't get over how beautiful you are," she said to her son as John snapped the camera. "You don't look like the usual wrinkled raisin. And you're so alert. Many people have been praying for you."

"You're the answer to our prayers," John added as he ran a finger along a miniature fist. "What do you think, is he a Peter Jeremy or an Andrew Michael?"

"Andrew Michael. Yes, that fits him best."

"I agree." John took his son in his arms again. "Andrew Michael, we love you and we've been waiting so long for you. Today you're coming home to live with Mommy and Daddy."

John and JoAnn had been left alone with their newborn son for a full half-hour before Ted and Linda joined them. They talked in general about the birth mother's family; then Ted cleared his throat. "You'll notice there is nothing stated about his father. This is a very special boy. He was conceived by rape. Will that make any difference?"

JoAnn instinctively held her son closer, and without even flinching John replied, "Not a bit."

"His birth family has sent along some letters," Linda explained. "I'll start with the one from his grandmother. It's dated one week before his birth."

Dear Mother and Daddy,
    I know this is one of the most exciting and happy times of your lives. On many occasions we have talked about how it would

be for you. We would even get excited for you. Not knowing who you were, we have talked about you and used our imaginations on the kind of people you are and how you would respond to the phone call telling you of a baby. Every day we have prayed for you. Even though we will not meet, I feel as if you are a part of our lives, as my own children. Be assured you will always be prayed for as will your precious baby, our first grandchild.

I remember the night my baby came to me and told me of her situation. She was so scared and distraught. For three months she had carried the burden of her pregnancy and the cause of it ... Of course, we felt as if our world had come to an end. There had never been such a devastating experience. The beauty is that immediately our Father's loving arms lifted us and reminded us that He would never put on us more then we could bear.

My husband has been a preacher since he was 15. We married young, ages 19 and 20. He has pastored churches since age 16. In all of our years of teaching and preaching we have never experienced what this past six months has allowed. We have claimed every promise in God's Word. We have experienced every feeling to be felt. We have cried and wept with heartbreak. We have drawn closer together as a family and to our Lord. Without His grace (II Corinthians 12:9) we could not have survived. We give Him the praise and thanksgiving. Yes, all things do work for the good, to them that love God, to them who are the called according to His purpose. (Romans 8:28)

I would like to share with you a little of your baby's birth mom. She is the youngest of our three children. Being from a pastor's home she was always in church and all the youth activities. She loved church ...

She has always been a very strong Christian with daily Bible study. She has continually been submissive in her attitude and spirit. She, of course, was normal with her teenage emotions, etc, but never rebellious. I have asked the Lord many times, why our daughter? One day He led me to Job 1:8-12. Then I understood a little of what God was doing in her life and ours.

One of the most difficult things in our life is making alternative future plans for our baby. It is only because we love it so dearly that we are able to do so.

First, we must think of our own daughter. She must go on with her life. Her desire is to finish high school and go on to college. It is not that she does not love her baby, because she does. It is because she knows she cannot be the mother that it needs. Every day she tenderly talks to the baby and tells it how wonderful its parents will be and how they are going to take care of it with all the love they have.

Secondly, I'm not ready to start again with children. The Lord wants me in the role of grandma and not mother. I love our baby as if it were my own. It is because I love it so, that I can also release it to someone else. Our baby deserves the best and we know you will give it the best.

This whole event has been a family thing. We have come together in support and love that I never dreamed possible. We all refer to it as "our" baby … You see, we have been preparing for nine months to give one of the greatest gifts a person could give — life — that life we give to you.

You will always be remembered in prayer as will (our) your baby. Ephesians 4:6-7 is one of those promises that has become a part of my daily walk with the Lord.

Would it be too much to ask for you to send this grandma a picture? I know that your own parents will be the "grandparents," but I think I could manage the birthdays, etc., better if I could see how he or she is maturing and progressing in life. This is my first grandchild and I'm very proud of it …

Birth Grandmother

P.S. Second request. Would you let us know when our baby accepts Jesus as his Lord and Savior. Matter of fact, we believe God has a special purpose for this child as with Hannah and Samuel. God Bless.

1/22/90 a.m.

Good Morning Parents,

Today is your big day. At this point you are not even aware of it. My heart fills with excitement for you. Tonight you will be parents of a beautiful boy.

For two days we have held and loved him. So sweet. He is a good baby. He has cried only twice. He has to be the most perfect baby.

Pray for us please. We have much to deal with. Our Lord will continue to strengthen us.

We love you,
Birth Mother.

"I prayed over and over," JoAnn said, wiping the corners of her eyes, "that our baby would be held and loved in the hospital."

"He was loved, I can assure you," Linda commented. "Now, here's the letter the grandmother wrote to your son."

Dear Child of my Child,

The day finally came for you to be born. January 19, 1990. What a beautiful day it was. Even though it was storming rain outside.

Your birth mother labored all day trying to have you natural. However, you just could not fit through the birth canal. At 5:30 p.m. your doctor told us a cesarean section would have to be done, so preparations began immediately.

From the very beginning I had promised your birth mother I would stay with her the entire time. What a beautiful experience! First, I saw your sweet little head come out and then your precious body. It was then I knew you were a boy. It was a sight I will never forget. In one view I could see my own little girl,

179

who had to become an adult too early in life, and also see you, the child of my child.

You are loved so dearly, and it is because of that love that we give you to your mother and daddy. You will always remain in my heart as my first grandchild. Maybe one day, if not on this earth, then in heaven, I will see you again.

I love you, your birth mother loves you, your mother and daddy love you. But more than any, Jesus loves you and died for you so that you could have life everlasting. It is because of Him that you live now.

Know that every day you will be prayed for.

I love you,

Your Grandmother.

John and JoAnn had passed the baby between them as he fussed slightly, thrusting his little fists into the air. JoAnn reached for a bottle of formula in the package from the hospital and attached a sterile nipple. When she was settled, John placed their son in her arms and watched him suck contentedly.

"I have two shorter letters here from his grandfather," Linda said shuffling her papers around. The first is dated January 20.

Dear Friends,

You are the new parents of the most beautiful little boy I've ever seen. You are so blessed. We are so very thankful that God has given him Christian parents.

This is not the way we intended things to be with our first grandchild but our God does all things well. (Romans 8:28)

Through the very difficult period of our daughter's pregnancy we have prayed specifically for several things and God has already answered some of those prayers. (Ephesians 6:18)

We prayed for strength for our daughter and ourselves — God's grace has been sufficient.

We prayed for a healthy baby and he seems to be just perfect. (I personally prayed for a boy and that God would use him greatly as a man of God.)

We have prayed for you more than I have ever prayed for anyone I didn't know. We prayed that you would be godly parents, teaching our grandson the principles of God's Word.

We know you will love your son in a special way and we are praying for you to have wisdom also. God has given you a priceless gift and a great stewardship of life.

We covenant to pray for you and your son in the years ahead. You were especially chosen by the Lord for a very great ministry in the life of this special child.

We look forward to photos and information about how he is doing. We will cherish that.

Your son's birth mother is a brave and beautiful young woman. We are very proud of her courage and faith.

We don't know you but we love you and we are happy for you. We look forward some day to seeing you — if not here, in heaven, and getting a full report.

In Christ,

Grandpa (Proverbs 22:6)

"This last short letter was written this morning," Linda commented, after she cleared her throat. "It's from the grandfather to his grandson."

You don't know me but I am the dad of your birth mother. She is a great gal and though it was tough for her, she loves you so much she gave you to your parents so you would have the love of mom and dad who could take care of you well.

Our little girl made a courageous choice not to have an abortion as a teenager so you could have life and your wonderful parents could have you. You are very special.

I pray for you every day. I pray that you will give your life to Jesus as your Lord and commit your life to His will. Truthfully, I prayed for you before you were born. I prayed for a boy and that you would be a great man of God.

So many people love you and have prayed for you. God must have something very special for you. You are loved.

Grandpa (Jeremiah 1:5, Joshua 1:9)

Euuuuugh! All this ssssweetness and liiiiight is making me sick. Everybody loooooves everybody else. All is forgiven. They've eeeeven forgiven Eeeeugene. How disgusssssting! Forgiving your enemieeeees!

Hooooow can I accooooomplish my eeeevil intents with aaaaall this icky, gooey loooove floating around?

Perhaps, neeeext time I will get an eeeeasier asssssignment.

February —
September 1990

T wila's friend, Amy Gean, drove her parents' van to Ft. Worth to haul Twila and her accumulation of possessions back to Ft. Smith. Moving back in with her parents delighted Twila, but her greatest thrill was a letter from the adoptive parents sent through the Hope Agency.

January 23, 1990
Dear Birth Mother,
   Yesterday, my wife and I received a most marvelous and perfect gift, whom we have named Andrew Michael. We can only begin to express our joy, elation and delight which we have shared the past twenty-four hours with this blessed child. We have prayed for many months and years for this event: for the health and welfare of the child; for the mental and spiritual strength of the birth mother; and, for our own abilities as future, Godly parents.
   Late last evening, my wife and I had our first opportunity to read the special letters, with your thoughts and those of your parents and the messages (which will be carefully stored and preserved for the future). From what has been shared, we know that yours is a special and close, Christ-centered family. How happy we were to hear that both you and your family were able to spend time with the child. It was important to us to know that Andrew went from one to another set of loving arms. We also know and understand that you and your family love this child so very much.

The darling blue outfit and soft blanket which clothed Andrew are beautiful. Already, he is dressed in fashion and style. We thank you so much for the clothing and will always remember and cherish the gifts that you sent. With the passing of our first day and night with Andrew, he surprisingly continues to be, thankfully, quiet with barely a tear. In fact, last evening he slept four straight hours, although the sleep did not begin until 3:00 a.m.

For now, it almost seems impossible that Andrew is with us, that at long last our prayer has been answered. Our prayers for you and your family will continue. May God bless you in your recovery from the Caesarean section and as you return to complete your education. We covet your prayers that God will guide us to be wise parents.

With Warmest and Sincere Love,
Andrew's Mommy and Daddy.

JoAnn enjoyed working in the church nursery even more after adopting Andrew. He was four weeks old when Mandy was taking her bi-monthly turn in the nursery. She rocked nine-month-old Ryan while clucking, "Poor thing doesn't weigh much more than a feather. But then Jody said his real mother was only fifteen and everyone knows teens live on coke and chips; he's probably malnourished. How much were you able to find out about Andrew's real mother?"

"Well, first off, I am Andrew's real mother. As far as his birth mother is concerned, John and I have chosen to keep the information we have about her for Andrew."

JoAnn didn't want to be offensive, but she always bristled when an insensitive person implied an adoptive mother wasn't the "real" mother. What did they think she was anyway, a lifetime baby sitter?

"And as to your theory on a mother's eating habits and her child's size, I'm not sure." JoAnn kept her voice casual as she gave her defense. "Nutrition, I'm sure, can be a factor but there's also several generations of hereditary factors involved, too."

"Well, maybe," Mandy shrugged. "Still, it seems like most adopted kids turn out bad. I mean — well, there's one family here at church. I won't mention their names, but you probably know who they are, and their adopted kids cause all kinds of problems." JoAnn knew Mandy's reputation as a busybody, so she listened quietly and played with the baby on her lap as Mandy rattled on.

"Did you hear Marshall's daughter is really causing her parents problems, and Mr. Marshall's on the church staff."

"And she's their biological child too, isn't she?"

"Yeah, I believe she is and you know ..."

"That's amazing," JoAnn cut Mandy off. "I can't understand — because there wasn't a reason for her to misbehave. If she'd been adopted, that would explain it."

JoAnn relayed the incident to John over dinner. "I don't want to become overly sensitive — I am in a way. But you know, you just have to make some people stop and think, especially when they talk that way in front of an adopted child."

N ear the end of February Twila received another letter from Hope. She skimmed along until she came to the parts about Andrew.

> ... I know there must be times when you wonder what or how Andrew Michael is doing. Please know that Andrew is doing well and appears to be quite happy.
>
> The recent update from the adoptive parents indicates that they are still overjoyed with the new addition to their family. They stated that he rarely cries and constantly smiles. He went to the doctor on 2-14-90 for his well-baby check-up and he weighed in at nine pounds and 14 ounces. The parents also report that Andrew enjoys being rocked, and generally sleeps approximately three hours at a time. The adoptive parents were excited to be able to have both sets of grandparents present when they dedicated Andrew Michael to the Lord before their church family ...

Twila quickly went to the enclosed pictures. "Oh, Mom isn't his smile beautiful."

"Yes, he is precious, and just look at those eyes ... "

The next day Emily sent a letter back.

> Feb. 20, 1990
> Dear Andrew,

```
    Yesterday was a big day for your birth
mother. It marked your one month birthday,
her first day back at school and her last
doctor's appointment. She got her insurance
to begin driving and she started exercising
to lose the tummy she got while she was
carrying you.
    When she came home from school, we had
another good mother-daughter talk about her
day and how she felt about it. We both thought
back over the last months and reflected on
the difficult times we've had, but all the
negatives turned quickly into positives when
we started talking about you. You have been
worth it all.
    Everyday our hearts feel more strongly that
God has a special purpose for your life. It
is because of Him and for Him that you were
given life. You are loved dearly.
    Your Other Grandmother
```

By the end of March, Emily had completed a rape counseling class in Ft. Smith Community College. Not only did she recognize that Twila had experienced all the classic symptoms of a rape victim, but some insights stood out clearly in her mind and she shared them with Ron. "Unless they are injured, or become hysterical, and most don't, raped women don't report being raped; instead, they totally deny it ever happened."

"Yet the police, at least here in Ft. Smith, wouldn't believe Twila because she didn't tell someone sooner?"

"Yeah, well, the point is, Ron, that if Twila had not become pregnant, she probably never would have told us."

"And that kind of trauma being bottled up inside would have done more damage to her life?"

"Exactly! The bottom line is, her pregnancy was really a blessing."

"You mean that by giving little Andrew life, her own life has been salvaged?" Ron shook his head in amazement. "It's always a wonder to me how marvelous God really is."

"Another thing. The usual pattern is for the rapist to stalk his victim for some time before the actual attack."

"Really? I had never heard that."

"I hadn't either, but it is something that needs to be shared. We should spread the word so that women, young women, girls, can all be warned that if they spot someone following them, or standing outside their homes gawking, or staring at them in some public place, they should be alarmed. They should not be alone, and if it continues they should notify the police."

Another helpful insight Emily shared with Ron was learning what made a man rape. "There's no real answer other than common patterns. They're angry and seeking revenge, their masculinity is threatened and they're seeking power or they are sadistic."

"Did the classes suggest any methods of treatment or a cure rate?" Ron asked.

"No. As a matter of fact, they say, 'once a rapist, always a rapist.'"

Twila found school more frustrating than ever. Many of her friends had gone on with their lives and she was the odd one left behind but Amy Nunly's friendship never wavered. The two went shopping whenever they had time from their school activities.

"Did I tell you that I ran into Steve James in the lunch room once last fall after you were in Ft. Worth?"

"No." Twila was still concerned about her rather timid friend who had been interrogated by the police. "What did he have to say?"

"It was right after the police had questioned him. I could tell he was fuming. He was so mad he was throwing his books around. I went over to him and tried to explain that you didn't accuse him but that the police were just doing their job."

"What did he say?"

"He just said you had no right. I don't think he ever got over it."

In spite of everything, Twila refused to let herself become defeated. "Mom," she said one day after school, "I gave my heckling speech today." She'd been preparing for days to give an assigned speech on a controversial topic. The assignment also required each student to prepare for a defense against heckling arguments from their classmates during the speech.

"Well, Twila, how'd it go?"

"Fine, but I didn't give it on what I planned."

"What did you give it on?"

"Pro-life in cases of rape."

Emily almost fell off her chair. "What did the class say?"

"They started to heckle me, so I told them my story."

"What did they say then?"

"Nothing. It got so quiet you could have heard a pin drop."

"What did you do?"

"I cried some." Twila went for a diet pop. "I'm glad I did it though, because some of the girls told me later that it really made them stop and think."

Twila never ceased to amaze her parents and it wasn't long before she surprised them again. "I've landed a part in the school play," she announced one evening over supper.

"Didn't you say they were doing *Sound of Music*?"

"Yes, and I'm a nun."

Emily about choked on her coffee. "Well if that isn't about the funniest thing I've ever heard of. The Baptist preacher's daughter, who's an unwed mother, is playing the part of a Catholic nun."

In March, Twila received another update from Hope with more pictures. Andrew was growing quickly and "enjoys being rocked and having stories read to him. He continues to be a sweet, easy-going baby." Each month updates and pictures were sent and in July the Herrods received a video. Emily immediately expressed her gratitude.

Dear Andrew and Parents,

Thank you is not sufficient enough for the tape of Andrew. We were all so excited I could hardly open the package quickly enough. Such joy and excitement we felt. Grandma cried, Grandpa had a look of pride, and birth mother felt such a sense of peace and love in again knowing she had done the right thing.

… We are all very proud of Andrew. We still feel God allowed Andrew to be born to be used in a very special purpose … Parents, we pray for you. Your responsibility is great! You and Andrew are loved,

Birth Grandmother

P.S. A note on your birth mother, for the first time in over a year, I see my real little girl coming out. Her face once again radiates with happiness and contentment. The comparison of her 16th birthday pictures with her 17th birthday pictures is unbelievable. You would not think she is the same person.

She is now living with her older sister in another state and plans to finish high school through video correspondence. We all feel at peace with her decision. She is happy, therefore we are happy.

John and JoAnn stood silently before the Judge as he scanned Andrew's final adoption papers. Their attorney and Ted Watson from the agency stood between them discussing Andrew's birth date. "January 19, 1990, your Honor."

"But I have here that Andrew Michael was born January 26, 1990." The judge handed the legal document across the bench and the attorney reached over to receive it.

Since JoAnn stood by the attorney, she turned slightly and scanned the document in his hand for the erroneous birth date. At the same time she noticed an unfamiliar name, Herrod, and assumed it was an attorney or doctor or other official.

Later, as John and JoAnn joyfully discussed the official event on their way home, JoAnn asked, "Have you ever heard the name Herrod?"

"No, why?" John didn't quite catch how she could shift from discussing their final adoption of Andrew to some strange name.

"Remember when the judge handed our attorney the document with the wrong birth date? Well, I glanced over to see for myself and I just caught a glimpse of the name Herrod. It just struck me as unusual. With all the names I see at work, I don't think I've even seen that name before."

Their discussion switched again to the adoption party John's mother had planned for that evening. John's whole family would be there, his brother and two sisters and the five children they had between them.

"Your mother's really been looking forward to this day, hasn't she, John?"

"Yes, for her it's a milestone. She hasn't said a lot but deep down she's been so afraid Andrew's birth mother could change her mind and take him back."

"Funny isn't it, that thought hadn't even occurred to me. I guess the letters they sent with Andrew and all — I've never felt the slightest threat of that happening."

The first of September was hard for Emily. Twila's friends had gone back to school for their senior year. Emily grieved for all the long-anticipated senior-year events that were no longer a part of Twila's dreams.

Emily missed Twila's sleepy morning grunts and her afternoon bursts of joy or disgust, depending on how her day at school had been. She missed the delightful but annoying habit Twila had of tucking her and Ron into bed at night. All the routine activities uniquely theirs were irretrievably gone. Cutting anger again threatened to unravel her peace and thread her days with dark strands of bitterness.

How many years would they experience the effects from that one life-shattering event a year and a half ago? She thought of the California earthquake and the multiple aftershocks. They seemed an apt comparison to the way their lives were continually being altered in ways not always visible. Again, Emily claimed aloud the familiar verse, " ... God works for the good of those who love him, who have been called according to his purpose."

She checked her calendar for the time of a wedding that afternoon and also noted it was Grandparents' Day. Emily stood and cried. "I'm angry and bitter again, Father, and I don't feel thankful for anything. Still, I thank you that Twila was raped, that we have a healthy grandson that's loved and cared for."

The day before, a yellow package-notice arrived in the mail, so Emily left for the wedding early enough to stop by the post office. *Junk mail*, she figured, but when she got the package, the return address was Missouri. The agency had forwarded something. Back in her car she opened the card first and read, "For Two Special Grandparents. The sentiment inside was special but Emily took even more comfort from the verse the adoptive mother had printed inside. "Our children too shall serve Him, for they shall hear from us about the wonders of the Lord; generations yet unborn shall hear of all the miracles He did for us."

"Oh, thank you, Lord," she cried as she dabbed tears and unwrapped another packet of pictures. It could have been Twila's impish smile and blue eyes that sparkled back at her. Andrew had her blonde hair, even his head tipped slightly to one side. He even had a trace of the shadowed, deep-set Herrod eyes.

Hugging the picture to herself with one hand, Emily hungrily devoured the contents of the enclosed letter.

```
Dear Andrew's Grandparents,
    I was so happy to hear how much your family
enjoyed the videotape. Andrew is growing so
quickly and we are happy to be able to share
his growth and progress with you ... He hasn't
quite mastered crawling on all fours but moves
```

very quickly doing the "G.I. Joe" crawl. Last Friday he pulled himself up in his crib to a standing position. I have never seen him look so proud. Our baby is growing into a busy little boy so fast!

We hope all continues to be well with your family. Has Andrew's birth mother settled into her new school situation? We pray that this will be a good year in which she will decide her further education. Please send her our love and prayers.

We hope this first Grandparents' Day is special for you both. My husband and I feel very blessed to include you in our continued celebration of Andrew.

With Love,
Andrew's Mommy.

A fresh surge of loneliness washed over her while she filled the pain of her empty heart with praise to God that the adopted parents shared so much of their son through letters. The videotape especially helped to fill the empty void that never completely stopped aching.

Three weeks after Andrew's adoption became final, JoAnn opened a letter from her long-time friend, Donna. She chatted about daily life, her kids, her husband and their church. "We've just finished a Family Life Seminar here. It was fantastic. If you ever get a chance to attend one, you won't want to miss it. I've enclosed a page from the *Baptist Standard* which lists the speakers. Thought you'd find it interesting."

JoAnn finished reading Donna's letter and started to read the page from the Southern Baptist newspaper of Texas. "Oh, my goodness," she said. Andrew's eyes followed his mother to the telephone, from the vantage point of his chair swing, too young yet to know the significance of her discovery.

"John, I know who they are."

"What do you mean?"

"I know who the birth grandparents are."

"I felt you would find out."

"But I didn't do anything yet. I just got a letter from Donna and she sent a page from the *Baptist Standard* about a seminar they went to. The speaker is a pastor, Dr. Ron Herrod. John, Herrod was the name ..."

"... you saw on the adoption papers in court," John finished, and then he chuckled. "We knew Andrew's grandfather had his doctorate and I doubt there are too many pastors in the convention with that name." He chuckled some more. "Sounds like they're rather public people, and if that's the case, we'd have run into them in a matter of time anyway."

By the time John came home from work that evening, JoAnn had even more details to share. "He's pastor of First Baptist in Ft. Smith, Arkansas but he has another seminar scheduled in Dallas and left a phone number to call — so I did."

"Rather a curious person, aren't you?" John smiled his approval.

"Do you think I'm invading their privacy?"

"No. You're not making any contact with them. What did you find out?"

"The lady I talked to was a Mrs. Seaborn. I think Dr. Herrod is staying with them, at least she seemed to know a lot about him. I guess he pastored a large church near New Orleans before going to Arkansas. He does a lot of revivals and teaches this Family Life Seminar. He's written a couple of books, has three children, a boy and two girls and the oldest one's married. Everything she said about the family fits the profile from the agency."

Later that evening John asked, "Didn't the agency say something about Dr. Herrod preaching on pro-life the Sunday after Andrew was born?"

"Come to think of it, I think they did. I wonder if his church is big enough to have a media department. Maybe I'll make another phone call tomorrow."

The next morning while Andrew contentedly amused himself on the floor, JoAnn picked up the phone. She scribbled the number down as the operator entoned it, then depressed the button on the telephone a couple of seconds before dialing. A moment later a friendly voice answered, "First Baptist Church."

"Media please."

"Certainly."

JoAnn heard the phone clicking. Now, at least, she knew the church was big enough to have a media department.

"Media, may I help you?"

"Would it be possible to have a tape of the sermon Dr. Herrod preached last January on National Right to Life Sunday? I believe it would have been January 21?"

"Yes, of course. Your address please?"

After JoAnn completed her call, she mailed off more pictures to Andrew's birth family. In days she heard back from the birth mother ...

To the Parents of Andrew Michael,

I want to thank you for all the pictures you've sent and for the ones you sent to my parents. He is a beautiful baby and is certainly growing.

Mom's mailed me all of the pictures except for the one of Andrew with the football. All the ones I have though are beautiful and every expression he was making, I make those same expressions often.

I have some of the pictures in a small photo album and I have some in individual frames which sit on top of my dresser. And every time I look at each picture, I get a sense of joy and I think of how much joy and happiness I felt when I first held Andrew and I realize how much joy ya'll have each day.

I am thankful every day for ya'll and thankful that God gave me strength to handle the situation. I also look forward every day to meeting you and to seeing Andrew again.

It has amazed me in the past few months how I can handle different trials without any difficulty because God gave me strength then and gives me strength now.

I loved the video. Having to do with the video, I have a small request. If ya'll have a video camera of your own and if ya'll feel comfortable with it, I would love to see when Andrew took his first steps. But I will understand completely if ya'll don't feel comfortable with that.

... My dad made a bribe with me last year that if I made all A's and B's along with all I went through, he would buy me a car. You see, I hadn't made the best grades my 9th and 10th grade years. So, I won the bet and he has bought a car.

I want to thank ya'll for all the pictures ya'll have sent. They are wonderful! As far as other pictures, ya'll do whatever ya'll feel comfortable with.

Well, I better go! Thanks again so much.

With love and prayers,

Andrew's Birth Mother

Emily wanted to make contact with the neighbor who had also been raped. She walked to her home several times but never found her, finally she resorted to phoning. "Betty, this is Emily Herrod," she identified herself. "I'd like to come over and visit with you for awhile because I'd really like to get to know you. I have a daughter named Twila and ... "

"Oh, yes," Betty interrupted. "The police have mentioned her to me but I didn't know where you lived and I thought you might not want to talk about it."

"Oh, but we do. May I come over?"

Betty stepped on a smoldering cigarette stub as Emily walked into the back yard. Once in the house and sitting down, she lit another. Emily gave no clue to the fact that she was highly allergic to tobacco fumes.

Betty smoked continually as she and Emily listened and shared. "Eugene had mowed my yard and done errands for me, so he had access to my house key." Betty took a long pull from her cigarette, exhaled and then snubbed it out. "He came in during the night when I was dead asleep. It was pitch dark. I suppose it was the same with your daughter."

"He must have been watching our house for some time because he seemed to have known Twila was all alone."

"I will tell you this." Betty blew a long stream of smoke from another cigarette. "I do not want Twila to go through what I've been through to make these charges. I went to the hospital, had all the humiliating tests. Let me make the charges. I'm forty-five years old, I can do it, but don't put her through it. She's been through enough. It is really bad."

"I'm sure you have had a hard time," Emily empathized. She realized how Betty's age was masked by her slender beauty and neat appearance. Emily could imagine the accusations Betty had faced during the questioning.

"When that trial comes up, I'll be there to support you in everything," Emily promised. "And when you're on that stand, I'm going to be right there with you. The trial starts September 5, doesn't it, Betty?"

"Yes, unless they change it."

"Are you sure, now, that you don't object to my being there?"

"Oh, no. I'd like to have you there."

Emily dressed in her Sunday best and arrived at the appointed time. "Ron," she began when she met him for lunch during the noon recess, "when I walked into that courtroom, it was like — I couldn't believe it. I could have spotted that guy anywhere. He wore slacks and a plaid shirt."

Emily sat alone all three days of the trial. Ron had made reservations for the weekend for them to attend a retreat for pastors and their wives but she couldn't make herself stay home to pack. "I can't leave to go on a retreat and not be there for Betty," she explained to Ron late Friday afternoon. "And I'm going to wait for the verdict." It wasn't long before he joined Emily in the courtroom and waited with her.

The prosecuting attorney talked to them briefly. "If Marrow's freed anytime soon, there's a one hundred percent guarantee he'll rape again, but if we can keep him in prison until he's thirty-five he may have a chance. And, like I said before, if we don't get a conviction on this trial, we will need Twila to make formal charges and do the DNA testing."

"If he is convicted, is treatment available for him in prison?" Ron asked.

"No, I'm sorry to say, there's limited help available."

Spectators and a few of Eugene's relatives milled around in the courtroom occasionally glancing anxiously at their watches. Ron noticed a man sitting slumped and alone, obviously disturbed. Ron walked over and introduced himself.

"Eugene Marrow's my boy. We haven't talked in ..." Clyde Marrow used the heel of his hand to wipe the tears from the deep groves in his face. "Well, it's been a long time. I've been gettin' counseling at the mental health center. He and his Maw don't talk neither. Things just never did go well between us."

Marrow looked older than his years. He sat with his elbows on his knees, clasping and unclasping his hands as he stared past Ron toward the jurors' room. "I'm sorry, really sorry, over what he did to your girl," he said, dropping his head into his hands, "But I don't want him to go prison neither."

"Mr. Marrow, please understand that my daughter, her mother and I have all forgiven your son. It's our prayer now that he will come to know the love and forgiveness of Jesus Christ. Let me explain ..."

Ron walked back to Emily, feeling only compassion for Mr. Marrow. "Twila can go on with her life, she'll recover — but their lives, Eugene and his parents are ruined."

"I hurt for his mother. It's her son and he'll live with this stigma the rest of his life. I can't help but think he's a victim, too."

Three and a half hours passed before the jury returned. Courtroom formality replaced the whispers as the judge read the verdict. Expressionless, he fixed his eyes on Eugene Marrow and in a voice heavy with the authority of the court declared, "The defendant is found guilty ..."

Emily made her last entry in her journal that night:

> At the close of three full days of testimony and trial, I feel as if the heaviest burden in my life was lifted. The very simple word "guilty" for some reason took away a feeling

of unfinished business in my life. To know
that the father of my grandchild, the rapist
of my daughter, was found guilty in a court
of law was one of the most refreshing events
in the last thirteen months. With such mixed
emotions I can honestly close the book and
put it on the shelf. Even though it will always
be a part of our lives it is put behind, up
and out of reach.

J oAnn looked at the clock when she heard the shower
running. It was 3:30 a.m. *Must have a project he's trying
to get done,* she figured and she rolled over and went back to
sleep. It wasn't uncommon for John to go to work early when
he had a major project to complete.

Both Andrew and JoAnn slept late and before she'd
completed her morning routine the mail arrived. She
recognized the tape that arrived from Arkansas and
immediately put it into the tape recorder. She listened as she
finished her work.

... The God of the Bible is a pro-life God ...
The Bible makes it very clear, "Thou shalt
not kill." This applies as equally to the
unborn child as it does to the developing
child, to the mature adult, to the senior
citizen."

In his opening comments Dr. Herrod shared a number of
startling statistics on abortion but for JoAnn the reality of
those statistics became particularly meaningful when he
said,

In Arkansas, thousands of babies are killed
in the abortion chambers in this state every
year.

JoAnn felt Andrew crawling around her ankles and tugging at her skirt to be picked up. She stooped and picked him up and hugged him close. Dr. Herrod's next words could have been her own.

How I thank God for the courage of young women who will have their babies and not have them aborted. I want you to know it is the easy thing to have an abortion. It is the hard thing not to have it. Thank God for those young women who have that courage.

On the statue in New York harbor it says, "Give me your tired, your poor, your huddled masses yearning to be free. Send these, the homeless, the tempest tossed to me. I lift my lamp beside the golden door." That's America. Yet we fill garbage cans with chopped up bodies of five-, six-, seven-month-old pre-born infants. If we don't stand on this issue, God will hold us accountable …

I want to applaud some folks today. I want to applaud physicians who won't give in to greed and refuse to practice abortions. I want to applaud men like Randall Terry who head up Operation Rescue … I want to applaud … those who have started pregnancy help centers …

And today I want to take personal privilege and applaud a very special young lady in my life.

JoAnn hit the stop button on the recorder and rewound the tape a couple of seconds. She settled Andrew on the floor with toys hopefully distracting him for a few minutes. Then she sat down at the table. She hardly dared to breath when she started the recorder again.

And on Monday, tomorrow, adoptive parents will hold in their arms a child …

JoAnn paused the tape again. She knew that Monday. It was the day she and John opened their arms to receive their newly born son, Andrew Michael. She wept. She wept for her joy. She wept for their sorrow. She couldn't comprehend how horrible Dr. Herrod's tomorrow had been, to see his daughter give up her very first child, to say goodby to his beautiful grandson.

JoAnn backed up the tape and listened again.

... adoptive parents will hold in their arms a child they've prayed for and asked God for for so long.

For that moment Dr. Herrod seemed to care beyond himself and comprehend the agony of John's and her infertility. When JoAnn heard the emotion that choked him, she wiped aways the tears that streaked her own cheeks.

Thank God. Thank God for those in our country and our city and our church who have the courage, the courage — the courage to say no to murder and yes to the Word of God.

JoAnn called John, convinced beyond a doubt, after she had listened to Dr. Herrod's tape, that she had found Andrew's biological grandfather. Subdued by deep emotion she said little. "I'll leave the tape and recorder on the table. I think you might want to hear it even if you get home late."

John dragged home from work over twenty-four hours later. Tired to the bone and emotionally drained, he likewise wept when he realized the miracle of Andrew's birth — how the convictions of the blood family had protected his life.

If we believe that life is made in the image of God then we believe that life is sacred ... How stupid to think that simply the exodus from the womb suddenly makes killing a murder. The unborn child is a human being.

... Human life began when God shaped Adam into His own image and breathed into him the breath of life and this life has been transmitted from generation to generation in an unbroken chain that links Adam and Eve to every child conceived in their mother's womb.

A chain that in some way links us. John felt so close to this man, a kinship deeper than blood. In some mysterious way John knew the benefit of this man's prayers and that Andrew's grandfather had been touched by John's prayers. Even if they never met, their lives were bound and blessed by their mutual Father, their God.

John ached with fatigue but his mind was alert. He took the tape recorder to the living room and collapsed into the overstuffed rocker in the living room, listening and agreeing with Dr. Herrod's theology and logic.

*[An] argument we hear a lot is, we don't
know when human life and personhood begins.
[I've] refuted conclusively that argument for
one who believes the Bible ... But for the sake
of argument, let's consider for just a moment
that we do not know when human life begins.
Wouldn't it make sense to wait until we do
know conclusively when life begins before we
kill 25 million unborn children?*

I want to applaud ...

John leaned forward, stopping the soothing motion of the
rocking chair and rubbed his burning red eyes.

*... to applaud a very special young lady in
my life who's had the courage to give birth
to a child though it brought great, great pain
to her. Though that child is the victim and
product of rape, she would rather have scars
on her body than scars on her spirit the rest
of her life.*

John hardly heard the rest of the tape. He could think
only of the young girl who not only laid aside her
overwhelming shame and stigma to give life to her son, but
also gave him up so that he could have a better life than she
could provide.

October —
December 1990

JoAnn put Andrew in his highchair, tied his bib under his chin and gave him his new spoon and fork to play with. Then she poured a little, weak ice tea in his new mug and sprinkled in a bit of sugar. With Andrew momentarily content, she read her letters.

Oct. 12, 1990
Dear Adoptive Parents,
Today my mom and I went to Universal Studio and we loved it. The exhibits and rides were wonderful. When we went into the stores, I always thought of Andrew. Of course, Mom and I had to buy something. I couldn't resist when I saw these things. I hope Andrew enjoys ya'll playing with the puppet and talking to him.
Please tell me if you object to me sending this. I usually don't and probably wouldn't have sent it, but I just couldn't resist. Maybe when he is 17, he can read this card and see what his birth mother gave him when she was 17. But, I also know ya'll have wonderful judgment.
I am thankful for ya'll every day. You have been such a blessing and have been so caring to my family. I know Andrew is a bundle of joy and I am praying for God to give ya'll strength and for Andrew's growth physically and spiritually as he gets older.
I've gotta go. Take care.
Love,
Andrew's Birth mother

J ust after Halloween Twila tore open a fat envelope from the Agency and quickly scanned the cover letter.

```
Dear Twila,
    It was so good to hear from you last month.
As usual it sounds as though you are keeping
busy with school and work. I hope that your
father will learn soon whether the church he
has explored with will call him as pastor.
```

Twila was more interested in reading the enclosed letter and studying the pictures from Andrew's parents. She had a letter written in return before she went to bed that night.

```
    Nov. 11, 1990
    Dear Andrew's Mommy and Daddy,
    I want to thank you for the pictures first
of all. They are so cute. It has amazed me
how much Andrew has grown. He is so big. And
you can certainly tell that he is in wonderful
health.
    I feel wonderful about Andrew and where he
is because I know he is taken care of, loved
and happy. As long as he remains happy, I will
be happy. I want the best for him … I am also
grateful that he is in a Christian home and
has Christian parents. I know that if we didn't
receive pictures or weren't able to
correspond, my emotions would be a basket
case.
```

What keeps me going every day is to see Andrew's picture in my room and to see how happy he is.

A few weeks ago, I did an interview on one of the local radio stations and I have a tape of it. I have mailed the tape because I want you to hear it. My first name is mentioned on the tape and that is the only revealing information. I don't mind you knowing who I am but I respect your privacy and don't wish to make you feel uncomfortable in any way. It does not matter to me or to my parents if you know who we are.

Well, I must go now. There is a present for Andrew in the mail that should get there soon. Thank you so much for the pictures. We appreciate you and pray for you and Andrew every day.

With Love
Andrew's Birth mother

J oAnn opened the door and was surprised to see Ted Watson from the adoption agency. "Hi, Ted, come on in." They talked for a few minutes and Ted commented on how much Andrew had grown before he approached the subject of his visit.

"I've a couple of things I need to mention. First, we've received a tape from the birth mother but it has some revealing facts so we will not be able to give it to you." Ted told JoAnn what he could remember of the tape.

"The other matter I came to mention is that we think you all are corresponding too much and for the sake of the birth mother you need to decrease the amount of contact to cards and letters, once or twice a year."

Neither JoAnn nor John had sensed any struggle in the letters from Andrew's birth mother, but eager not to complicate problems she asked, "Have you explained to her that it's not us stopping the correspondence?"

"Oh, yes, certainly."

"I have this real uneasy feeling, John," JoAnn explained later that evening. "All their letters talk about how much they like the pictures we send and how much they appreciate knowing about Andrew. His birth mother has said over and over again it's the letters and pictures of him that keep her going. Besides, they all wanted us to have that tape."

"Seems her parents would know how she's doing better than the agency."

John studied his wife as she talked. He could almost see her strong will flexing like a boxer before a fight. He knew she was determined to get the tape. What would be the harm as long as there was not direct contact? Knowing he didn't have a good strong argument to counter her's, he looked at her and smiled. "Tradition dictates we don't make contact but in my heart I'm really open to letting the grandparents know what's going on with their grandson."

John and JoAnn discussed their dilemma continually the next few days. "Wonder what Hope would do," John asked while at the dining table one evening, "if they knew we have located Andrew's birth family?"

"But it was all a chain of circumstances. I didn't purposely set out to see the Herrod name on those legal papers in court."

"And since the adoption is final, legally we're free to maintain or stop contact as we see fit."

"It's the idea of knowing what's best for the birth family that concerns me; which will bring the most emotional healing." JoAnn sat at the kitchen table with her chin in her cupped hands. "Every letter from them has been so appreciative."

"If we made contact, the other risk to consider would be if Hope found out and we'd hurt our chances of adopting more children." As grateful as JoAnn was for Andrew, he couldn't fully satisfy her childhood dream of having seven children.

John scooped a generous serving of hand-packed praline ice cream into dishes for the two of them. "What about finding a neutral party that would be willing to make contact with just the grandparents? Dad knows people throughout the whole denomination."

The idea of a third party contact sounded good for a few days but they both had one major concern. JoAnn brought it up.

"Let's say a third party makes a contact with Andrew's grandparents and they make a decision and later his birth mother finds out. Even if she agrees with their decision, how will she feel about being left out? What would it do to the relationship between her and her parents, or her confidence in us?"

The Taylors were willing to risk their future with the agency but the risk for Andrew's birth family was too great. They waited and continued to pray for the birth family, for their emotional strength and healing but still they weren't fully at peace with the agency's position.

E mily waved one last time to Ron as he walked out the double doors leading to the plane on Thanksgiving morning. He'd fly to Mobile for the day and meet Twila there. She was driving in from Florida. Friday they'd drive back to Ft. Smith together.

"I still have a few things to finish in her room and I'd rather have the time to myself." Emily had explained to Ron a couple of weeks before over their breakfast of cereal and coffee.

"Sort of hate to leave you behind for Thanksgiving."

"Twila's collected so many things there won't be room for all three of us in her car."

"Well now, that I can imagine." Ron smiled a knowing smile over the rim of his coffee cup. "I'm not too sure I feel good about you being alone overnight."

"Oh, I'll be fine." Emily didn't feel quite as brave as she sounded. "Besides," she reasoned, determined to overrule her emotions, "I can start getting ready for Christmas before Twila comes home and I won't be tired from the trip and have it all to do later."

"If you're sure that's what you really want to do, Em, I guess it'll be fine."

Twila wasn't as easily convinced. "Mom, you'll be alone all night by yourself."

"Now, Twee Dee, I'll be just fine," Emily used her most convincing voice. "It's only one night anyway."

"Just the thought of being alone in that house gives me the creeps. Are you sure you want to?"

"Yes, Twila. And now don't you worry about it."

"I will worry but we'll call and check up on you."

Emily shuddered briefly at the realization that Eugene had watched Twila from under the cover of darkness only a couple of feet from where Emily now stood. She felt relief as she hung blinds and curtains over the window, double checking to make sure they fully covered the entire expanse.

With a greater sense of security, she rearranged the furniture in Twila's freshly painted room, made her bed with fresh new linens and spread a brand new comforter over the top. Emily put only a couple of new wall hangings up, enough to take the sterile look from the room and give it a welcome feeling. Twila would have others with her.

Emily felt so good about Twila's room, she decided to change a few things in the family room. It was late and dark when she stood again at the top of the stairs. Suddenly she felt as if her heart had stopped. *Okay, Emily, you're going to go downstairs tonight by yourself. You're not going to let fear get control of you.* She took a deep breath. *You're going to have control of the situation.*

As she went downstairs she remembered Ron's painted mallard duck telephone she'd given him for Christmas a year before. Although he had it in his office he never used it, so she steeled herself against the phantom presence lingering in the silent family room and walked directly to Ron's office. Giving the phone a light dusting, she hooked it up on the table at the end of the couch. She liked the quaint effect.

Emily talked aloud to herself off and on throughout the evening as she moved some of the furniture around and cleaned the entire room. She wanted to create a different look, anything to mute past memories. It was 11:30 p.m. before she sat down in the glow of the fireplace, satisfied with her efforts.

If it weren't for that door. Emily knew it was locked but the door was such a stark reminder. *That's where he came in.*

"Quaaack, quaaack. Quaaack, quaaack." Emily jumped to her feet as a pang of terror shot through her. "Quaaack, quaaack. Quaaack, quaaack." Emily looked quickly around the room. Two small beads of light flashed. She stifled a sob. Tears spilled down her cheeks. "Quaaack, quaaack." Blink, blink. "Quaaack, quaaack." Blink, blink.

"Oh!" Emily remembered the phone. "You dumb duck." By the time she crossed the room and reached for the phone she was so relieved she couldn't talk. She half laughed and half cried into the receiver.

"Em, is that you?" Ron's voice barked loud with concern. "Are you all right?"

"Your duck came to life."

"My what?"

Emily related her frightening moment between bursts of laughter. Laughter which didn't fully relieve Ron's momentary shock at hearing his wife's hysterical "hello." He no longer felt secure leaving his family in Ft. Smith.

J oAnn tied the Dino bib under Andrew's chin and put his Dino sippy cup on his tray in front of him. Suddenly her eye fixed on the Universal Studio signature on his bib and cup. *Orlando. Why didn't I think of it before?*

She reached for a scratch pad and pencil with one hand and the telephone with another and quickly dialed information. "Operator, would you please give me the names and phone numbers of all the radio stations within a fifty mile radius of Orlando?" By supper time she'd called her way down a long list of stations but found no clues about a radio interview of a rape victim.

JoAnn rolled restlessly beside John that night. By morning she'd decided on another plan and as soon as her morning work was done she dialed the operator again. "I'd like a list of all the Baptist churches in the Orlando area please?" As she started down her list of over thirty names she asked to speak to the youth minister. An hour and a half later David Gibson, youth minister at Trinity Baptist Church, promised to send her a copy of the tape.

JoAnn felt as if she knew Twila as soon as the program host introduced her and she began talking. "I was 15 ... at home alone one evening ... I felt embarrassed and ashamed, that I wasn't worth anything, so I didn't tell my parents or anybody.

"I did think about abortion, but not for very long because I'd always, in discussions in and out of classes, I was always against abortion. But when you face the situation, I did think about abortion. I'm thankful now I didn't have one.

"... After I told my parents they said there are many couples waiting to adopt babies right after they're born ... I realized that was the best decision because, not only was it the best decision for me, but the best decision for my baby. He would have a father that way. And he would have a wonderful family, grandparents, uncles, cousins ... "

"What was the reaction of the Christian community?" the host queried.

Twila explained the difference between the friendly open people in New Orleans and the reserved cliques in her new hometown. "Most of the adults accepted it in the church. There's a certain group, of course, that is always going to think, 'she wasn't raped, she just went out and got into trouble and everything.'

"I think for the youth group — it was hard for them to take because after I had the baby and went back to Arkansas, it was hard for them to accept it and for me to get accepted back into the youth group." Twila's voice was clear and sweet, without anger or hatred.

"... I had my mom there because through this whole situation, Mom and I grew closer."

"... I felt like nobody, no one's going to love me, no one's going to accept me anymore. I had to ... learn that it really didn't matter what other people think ..."

For four-and-a-half years the Taylors prayed for the mother of their child. Now JoAnn had heard her voice and that her name was Twila. She felt a kinship, a love, a trust — being the mother of this young woman's son. *Can I bond with someone through prayer whom I've never met*, she wondered?

Twila looked forward to finishing the Christmas decorating, but first she had unpacking to do.

"I'll fold the clothes, Twila, while you unpack and then we'll start."

"Okay, Mom." Before she got halfway across the family room the phone started ringing. "I'll get it." A few minutes later she joined her mother in the laundry room.

"You don't look too happy, Sweetheart. Is something wrong?"

"That was Linda from Hope. She thinks it's really something that we're still getting so much correspondence from Andrew's mother."

"I know, hasn't it been wonderful. They've been so generous, all the pictures and everything."

"Linda said not to expect much more correspondence from them." Twila tipped her head to the side. "She said that last month, come to think of it." Twila started matching socks. "I guess she wanted to remind me they weren't obligated to send pictures more than once a year."

"They haven't been obligated to send so many pictures and letters either. They've been more than generous."

"That's just it. Linda said to be prepared for them not to send anything at all."

"But they've been so generous with sending stuff so far that surely they'd send stuff after his birthday, too?" Emily put a stack of folded clothes in Twila's arms.

"That's what I said, but Linda said not to expect anything."

"Now, Twila, I just can't imagine that." Emily picked up another stack of clothes. "I guess we'll just have to wait and see."

Emily and Twila finished decorating the entire house before the first of December. The living room tree reflected Emily's artistic flare, the tree in the family room reflected her love for her family and tradition. Handmade decorations from each child's childhood and their own collections of novelty ornaments — all held special memories.

A new stocking identical to Twila's hung on the mantle. Emily had made it. After Twila hung it she ran her fingers lightly over the letters, *ANDREW*. For a brief moment she could almost feel his tiny warm body in her arms again. That night she wrote her son a letter and in the morning she mailed it, along with two others.

J oAnn was surprised to see Ted Watson at her door so soon again. "Looks like you're about ready for Christmas," he said cheerfully as he followed her into the livingroom.

"Nearly," she answered, "but these boxes aren't coming, they're going. Andrew and I are leaving the ninth for Seattle. John will join us for the weekend and we'll have an early Christmas there with my family. Then we'll spend Christmas Day here with John's."

As they sat down, Ted handed JoAnn an envelope with the agency's return address in the upper left hand corner. "Christmas letters from Andrew's birth family," he said. "They also sent a picture we thought you'd like to see," and he pulled an 8" x 10" photo from a manila folder.

JoAnn froze as she gazed at the picture. Never had she been so startled. She'd never seen a picture of Andrew's birth mother, didn't even know she had blonde hair. She must have been the same age as Andrew when the picture was taken. They looked nearly identical.

"We'll place this in Andrew's file," Ted said as he took the picture from JoAnn's hand and slid it back into its folder.

"Why?" she asked, confident it had been sent for her to keep.

"Hope will decide when Andrew can see it." Ted cleared his throat and stood, about to leave. "One more thing, JoAnn, the agency has one other concern. We don't feel the birth mother is progressing emotionally as she should, so we want all correspondence to end."

"Have you told her parents?" JoAnn could hardly believe what was happening. *The agency has read all the letters. Couldn't they see how much the Herrods want to maintain contact? How could Hope make such an arbitrary decision, when the agency had no jurisdiction over any of us anymore?*

"Have you explained it's not us wanting to stop contact? I mean, what's going to happen in twenty years if we meet and this bitterness has formed because we've just stopped contact?"

"We're going to tell them we're doing it," Ted reassured.

"How can the agency decide about a picture the grandmother sent to us?" JoAnn was obviously upset. "We're his parents."

It took a lot to make John upset but when he heard the recent decisions of the agency he, too, was angry. "We should be able to decide when Andrew needs to see that," he agreed. Together they found comfort in the letters Ted had delivered. JoAnn rocked Andrew and John read aloud.

Dear Andrew,

This Christmas will be special for both of us. Not only do I think about you every day, but I will be thinking of you even more this Christmas.

I know you will have a wonderful Christmas and that you will receive numerous gifts and toys. But I pray that when you are older, you will come to know Christ as your personal Savior and also come to realize the true meaning of Christmas, which is the birth of Jesus Christ.

This Christmas we are making you your very own stocking to hang over the fireplace. We are also opening a savings account so instead

of giving you a gift each year, we will put
money into the account. When you are older
the money from the account will help to pay
for things.

I pray for you each day, Andrew. You are
always in my thoughts and I will always love you.
        With Love,
        Your Birth mother.

With Andrew on her lap and listening to the letters as
John read them aloud, JoAnn became even more convinced
that to deny Andrew all knowledge of his family heritage
couldn't be right.

She said nothing, but she took the letter when John
handed it to her and tucked it into Andrew's pink, little
hand. She wanted him to have all that he could of his birth
mother. Andrew babbled softly and rattled his letter while
JoAnn leaned her head back against the rocker and listened
to John read aloud the second letter received that day.

Dear Andrew,
        Christmas is always the most special time
of the year for us. This year it is even more
special because we were all blessed this past
year with you. This has to be the most exciting
Christmas for your parents too.

Even though you are not with us in person
you will always be in our hearts. Your stocking
will hang by the chimney along with all the
others. I made it special for you and had your
name monogrammed on it like your birth
mother's.

Andrew, we love you and your parents. We
are praying for a very Merry Christmas for
you and your entire family.

        Hugs and kisses to you, my little grandson,
        Gremmy

P.S. "Papa" and "Gremmy" will be our call
names for our grandchildren. You are the first
to use it.

John blinked tears from his eyes as he handed the letter
to JoAnn. She pointed to the picture on the stationery, "Tree,

deer. Andrew, see the tree and the deer? See the rabbit? There's even a little raccoon." Andrew spread his chubby little fingers, poked at the paper and babbled. John began reading the next letter.

Dear Andrew,

We are thinking of you and praying for you on your first Christmas! This is a special time because the baby in the manger was God and He came in the Person of His Son to die on the cross for our sins. We celebrate because He arose from the dead and is alive today.

We are praying that you will receive Him as your personal Savior at a very young age.

We are also praying that your first Christmas will be the most wonderful your parents have ever experienced.

We realize that you will receive more gifts than you know what to do with this year. So your birth mom is opening an account for you at the bank. She has a job for the Christmas season & is using some of it for your savings account. It is to help with your education later on. We love you. Merry Christmas.

Papa

January 1991

Twila had thought of Andrew often through the holidays and now she and Emily decided to have a birthday party. "That way we can have pictures to send to Andrew and he'll know he wasn't forgotten."

On January 15, Twila wrote a short note to Andrew's parents.

> ... I want the two of you and Andrew to know that my family and I are thinking about and praying for ya'll.
>
> This first birthday will be special for all of us. We are going to have our own family celebration here for Andrew and I know ya'll will have one in MO.
>
> Enclosed in Andrew's card are a few pictures of Christmas. I have signed one of my many nicknames from my parents, "Twee Dee," because we don't want Andrew to become confused when he is older.
>
> We love ya'll and are praying that this will be a wonderful year for ya'll.
>
> With love,
> Andrew's Birth mother,
> "Twee Dee"

JoAnn dated her only permitted letter for the coming year, January 21, 1991.

Exactly one year ago tonight I sat in our nursery rocking the most precious baby in the world. I cannot believe an entire year has passed. Tonight as I rocked Andrew to sleep I remembered the excitement and joy we felt when he arrived.

... Three days ago when we celebrated his first birthday, I thought that I didn't even know about him a year ago. I will always be so thankful for you giving him lots of love and attention after his birth.

... I was shocked to see your baby picture. I could not believe the resemblance. You and Andrew could not look more alike. If you would not mind, I would love to have a recent picture of you. The agency kept your baby pictures for Andrew's file but I would love to see any more your mother would like to send.

... I also hope you will remember how wonderful and special we think you are. You have not only given us the gift of Andrew but you have also been so lovingly willing to communicate with us ... I want you to know that as Andrew continues to grow, we will show him the many letters and tell him of your love for him. I will always hope that we will all meet when he is older but if he decides not, I will still know you through the time we have written this past year.

In His love,
Andrew's Mommy and Daddy

Since Andrew's birthday on the nineteenth, and writing to Andrew's birth mother, JoAnn had had no peace. All she'd been able to think about was Ron Herrod's taped message from the previous year's National Right To Life Sunday.

Monday evening, over the remnants of Andrew's birthday cake, she shared her feelings with John. "I keep wondering if Dr. Herrod might have said something else about his daughter or grandson. I wonder what his feelings might be now, after a year."

"I've kind of wondered the same thing." John's voice lacked the intensity of his wife's. Since they hadn't thought of a suitable third party, and didn't feel free to write the grandparents, they'd given no further consideration to any kind of direct contact with the Herrod family.

Thursday morning JoAnn was even more restless. "I just can't get Dr. Herrod off my mind."

"It would be nice just to see him."

"I can't help but think how good it would be to be able to tell Andrew someday, 'Yes, we've seen your grandfather and heard him preach.' We could even take pictures of his church."

"If we're not going for the purpose of making contact, I don't suppose there's any harm. We could give it some thought."

JoAnn had thought — all week. It was Thursday, she'd call Ft. Smith.

"Sunday's going to be Dr. Herrod's last day here in Ft. Smith. He's accepted a call to another church in Tennessee," the receptionist informed her.

"Thank you, I appreciate your help." JoAnn's hand shook with excitement as she placed the phone in its cradle. She waited only a few seconds before dialing her husband's work number.

"John, it's me. I just called First Baptist Church in Ft. Smith and you'll never believe what I just found out."

"Try me." John had ceased being surprised by JoAnn's impulsive actions. JoAnn quickly related her news. "If we're going to see them and hear him preach, it's got to be this weekend because Andrew hates traveling too much for us to drive clear to Tennessee."

"Well, we've been saying we're going to go up there sometime and just look around. It would be good to hear him preach."

"The last pictures they've seen of Andrew were the ones I sent after Halloween. He's changed so much in the last three months, if they should see him, they wouldn't recognize him."

"Can you be ready to leave early Saturday morning?"

Twila, you've got to get up." Emily was talking as she stepped quickly down the stairs. "The packers will be here shortly and we've got to be ready to leave early Monday morning."

Ron had accepted the call to Central Baptist Church in Oak Ridge, Tennessee a couple of weeks earlier and now with only Friday and Saturday left before their actual moving day, there was much to get done.

Twila was sitting straight up in bed, wide awake and smiling. "Mom, you won't believe what I dreamed." Emily expected the usual, sleepy moan from her daughter and was startled to see her usually half-opened eyes radiant with excitement.

"I dreamed I had Andrew here for a week and took him to church. I played with him on the floor and he crawled to me."

"Well, Twila, how nice. He probably is crawling by now."

"Mom, it was so wonderful, it was all so clear."

"Who knows, Sweetheart, maybe the Lord gave you that dream for some special reason." All day Friday and again Saturday, Twila talked in detail about her dream and Emily listened, believing God was giving comfort for some special need or emptiness Twila must have felt.

Excitement kept both John and JoAnn talking until late Friday night. "Even though it isn't our stated purpose to meet them, I suppose it's possible, so I think if anybody asks his name, let's just say Andy."

"I have no problem with that," JoAnn replied, stifling a yawn. "Then if they have any suspicions they can ask more questions or remain anonymous. The decision will be up to them."

"Another thing." John's voice was getting sleepy. "Everyone seems to ask a baby's age. Let's not give any dates. We'll just say he's a year old." Finally, at peace with their plans, they both fell asleep.

The Taylors left St. Louis at 4 a.m. the next morning. Over breakfast in Lebanon, Missouri, they finalized their plans for the weekend. "I think we should drive by the church and if it's small, one of us should stay at the motel with Andrew in the morning and then switch off for the evening."

"I'll buy that. If it's large we can both go; we'll be lost in the crowd. But I do think we should keep Andrew with us so we don't have to fill out visitor forms. Besides, the way he's been acting lately, he's not about to go to any stranger."

"So you think he's bonded well enough?" John flashed a smile at his wife and they both grinned. He knew how important bonding was to them both and now, typical of any child, Andrew had reached the stage where he wouldn't go to strangers.

"Bonded like super glue, I'd say, and I love it." JoAnn turned in her seat and handed Andrew a soda cracker. "Do you think we'll have time to scout out the Herrods' home? We should be able to get their address in the telephone directory."

"If all goes well, we should be in Ft. Smith by mid-morning," John said as he looked at his watch. "We should have time to do that before we check in at a motel."

The Taylors felt a mixture of excitement and apprehension as they neared the outskirts of Ft. Smith but JoAnn, as usual, was first to put her feelings into words. "You know, John, I keep wondering what kind of people they are. Some Christians are happy regardless of what happens in their lives and others go through life moaning about how much God has given them to bear. Just being able to see the Herrods should tell us a lot."

A few minutes after entering the Ft. Smith city limits they found the Herrods' home. "I'm sure that's it but it sits down off the road so far it's hard to see." JoAnn twisted in the car seat as John drove slowly by. "Let's drive by again."

After several passes John concluded, "Anybody looking out a window would wonder whose black car is creeping by the house."

"We've seen about all we can see anyway. It looks like they'd be comfortable people to be around," JoAnn concluded. Andrew was hungry and tired of his car seat and she handed him another soda cracker. "Let's find a motel and settle him down some."

John backtracked to a motel he'd seen earlier. Andrew crawled around on the bed while JoAnn arranged their things and John got directions to the church.

J oey, still damp from his morning shower, pulled on jeans, a faded t-shirt and tennis shoes. He skipped shaving and headed for the kitchen in his bachelor apartment and scarfed down a bowl of Almond Crunch. He packed light — shaving gear and clothes for Sunday — and started the four-hour drive from Oklahoma to Ft. Smith. The weather was cold and he wasn't feeling too well but he needed to go. It was his parents' last Sunday.

Joey cruised along between 75-80 mph on Interstate 40 and shortly before noon slowed to 35 before he crossed the Garrison Avenue Bridge into Ft. Smith. *From 70 to 35 when you cross one bridge. How symbolic of the difference in the mental attitude of this town.* He drove on down Garrison, past the old buildings, shifting constantly at one frustrating stop sign after another.

Impatient and a little warm, he rolled down his window and noticed a black Volvo, relatively new, with dark tinted windows, different from any other car he'd seen in Ft. Smith. *Driving through from Missouri. Sharp looking, yuppie type.* Joey could see a baby in the back seat and a lady in the passenger side studying a map and looking thoroughly confused.

John had driven for fifteen minutes and still couldn't find the church. As he rolled to yet another stop, he noticed a young fellow in the car next to them with his window down. "Ask this fellow."

JoAnn quickly rolled down her window. "Can you tell me where the First Baptist Church is, please?"

Joey hesitated a moment. "Which one?"

"The one that's somewhere around here."

"Okay. It's hard to give directions to it. Why not follow me? I'll go by it." He watched the Volvo pull in behind him and he snaked his way along the one-way streets the short distance to the church, wondering the whole time what someone from Missouri would want at First Baptist Church. He pulled into the church parking lot, expecting them to follow but instead they drove past him and began slowly circling the church, so Joey followed until they pulled up and stopped. The driver stepped out as Joey pulled along side. He switched off the ignition and opened his door. As he climbed out he flashed a friendly smile and offered his hand.

"Hi, my name's Joey Herrod. It's funny you should pull me over, because my Dad's the pastor of this church." Joey watched the blood drain from the man's face, his expression freeze and his chin drop. *Wow. Get a grip, man.* Joey didn't know what to say.

"Oh. Uh." The stranger stammered. "Oh, good." He shook Joey's offered hand, then stepped back, stammering. "John Taylor. Oh, well, uh, thank you. Okay. Well, we were just here in town and uh — wanted to know of a church to go to."

"Well, good. Hope you can make it tomorrow." Joey waved, got in his car and headed for home. By the time he arrived he'd drawn his own conclusions. "Hey, Mom, Dad, I think I've met the guy that's going to follow you. He's going to be the next preacher here. You know a guy named John Maylor or Taylor or something? Sharp looking car." Joey told his parents of the couple he led to the church. "They were so strange. When I introduced myself he just sort of looked at me and didn't say anything." Joey stood with his hands hooked halfway into his pockets. "Weird couple."

"Where were they from?" Emily asked.

"Missouri. Has the church called someone else?"

"Not that we know of." Ron leaned against the kitchen counter with a coffee cup in his hand, shaking his head.

He had no clue as to who we were," John said once he'd gotten his color back and could talk again.

"Do you think he looked in the car?"

"No, nothing other than maybe to see that you were in here."

The Taylors rehashed the incident all afternoon, while they waited for Andrew to nap and later as they wandered through a local mall.

"I just can't get over it, running into Dr. Herrod's son."

"I wonder what the laws of probability would be of that happening?"

"I don't have the faintest idea but I'm sure of one thing." JoAnn was pushing Andrew in his stroller. "If we had to go home right now, I'd be satisfied. Their son was so warm and friendly, just seeing him says so much about the family."

Twila and Emily dreaded their last Sunday at church in Ft. Smith. "Daddy says we need to be there, Twee Dee, and although I hate to admit it, he's right." Emily opened a box of doughnuts and poured herself a cup of coffee.

"We're supposed to be loving and gracious, even when we know some of the people are glad to see us go."

"I s'pose so," Twila agreed grudgingly. "Besides, Dad said I could sing tonight and it wouldn't look too good if I stayed home this morning and went to sing my testimony tonight." She opened a diet soda and reached for a doughnut. "That reminds me, there's a Sunday school dinner after church. I thought I'd go."

"Oh, Twila. Please don't. Joey has to leave right after lunch and this will be the last time we can be together for a long time. It's been so hectic these last few days and it's important to Daddy and me that we have a family lunch together, just the four of us." Twila agreed.

A short time later, Twila, armed with her curler and make-up bags, went with Ron to church. Emily and Joey followed later. As they drove into the parking lot, Joey commented, "I wonder if that couple made it to church this morning."

Emily enjoyed having Joey and Twila beside her in church. Immediately after the benediction, Joey turned to her. "I'm going to go find that couple."

"Well, go ahead and see if you can find them." *Boy is he obsessed with that couple.* Emily watched Joey for a moment then turned her attention to Twila. "Sweetheart, go on over to Holiday Inn and get seats for us at the restaurant." Twila left the church from a side exit, grateful for a reason to leave immediately. Emily stood with Ron at the front as people filed by to express their goodbyes.

She easily recognized Joey from the remaining knots of people and couldn't help but smile. He'd apparently found his "weird couple" and stood there chatting away with them. She could see they had a baby.

The Herrods had only one person left to talk with when Emily glanced toward the back of the auditorium. Joey was gone and the couple was walking toward them. Emily admired the baby, thinking he looked so cared for in his blue coat and matching cap. She smiled as they stepped up to her.

"We're John and JoAnn from Missouri." JoAnn shifted the baby to one arm and offered her hand to Emily just as Ron spoke up.

"We're so grateful to have you folk with us today." Ron offered his hand. "I hope you enjoyed the service."

"We did, very much." John felt incredulous being so close to Andrew's family.

Emily's attention focused on the baby's blue eyes. *Eyes like his dad's,* she thought.

"And this little fellow?" Ron asked in his usual, friendly manner. "What's his name?"

Emily studied the baby. He turned his head and she walked around behind JoAnn, mesmerized — drawn.

"Andy," JoAnn answered according to their prearranged agreement, the moment swelling with anticipation. All her previous thinking flashed through her mind. They could pick up on his name, ask his age, his birthdate, more questions if they wanted to. Still, if they suspected "Andy" to be their grandchild they could choose to remain anonymous. They could also choose to reveal ...

"How old is Andy?" Ron's questions followed each other with no particular thought other than to offer friendship and establish a point of common interest.

"Andy's a year..."

Emily's thoughts raced, retrieved impressions and flashed pictures in her mind. That voice again — the videotapes — the baby — Andrew Michael — her grandson. Before JoAnn could finish, Emily in a voice softened by awe and wonder, completed the sentence "... and he was born January 19, 1990."

Emily reached out her arms for Andrew as JoAnn turned and said, "Yes, this is your grandson, Andrew Michael." Totally uncharacteristic of his last six weeks, Andrew tumbled eagerly into Emily's arms.

As Andrew Michael buried his beaming smile in Emily's neck and Ron witnessed her joyful hysteria, he began to comprehend. That moment it seemed as though heaven opened up and God reached down His hand and whispered, "Here's your grandson. I'm restoring what the locusts have eaten."

Instantly overwhelmed, tears started rolling down Ron's face as he stammered, looking to John, then to JoAnn and back to Emily and Andrew again. "Thank you, oh, thank you.

It's an answer to prayer. Thank you, this is so giving of you. It's so great of you all." Without waiting for answers he began asking questions. "How long have you known? How did you find us?"

Joey had re-entered the rear of the auditorium in time to see his mother holding the baby and sobbing, his Dad bouncing around, stammering with an expression of absolute joy and wiping his eyes. As Joey took in the scene before him, realization dawned. "Oh, my God," he prayed, incredulous with unbelief. Ron was cradling the baby when Joey stepped into the circle.

"I just figured out what's going on here." Joey looked the little guy over. His nephew, his sister's baby — so different from the tiny, wiggling bundle Joey had hesitated to hold a year ago. The innocent baby he'd been afraid to love, because he never expected to see him again, was now a blue-eyed smiling boy.

Joey didn't know what to do with his feelings, his thoughts. This wasn't supposed to happen. What would happen now, a year from now, years from now? He watched his mom, then his dad. He saw their joy. It had been nearly two years since he'd seen them so happy.

"Do you mind if Twila sees him?" Emily asked.

"No, but how will she take it?" John questioned. "She's been our biggest concern."

"Are you sure she's ready to meet Andrew?" JoAnn echoed.

Emily remembered Twila's dream and the Lord seemed to be saying, "Okay, she's ready. Go on. Take him."

"Twila will be fine. You can join us for lunch." Emily took Andrew again, oblivious of her red eyes and smeared mascara. "Twila's saving us a table at the Holiday Inn. Give us a couple of minutes and we'll prepare her."

Twila noticed her mother wiping tears as her parents walked toward her. When Emily reached the table her crying was more obvious. "Mother, why are you crying? We're leaving, you ought to be excited."

"Twila, I am excited. These are the happiest tears I've had in months."

"Well, what's wrong?" Twila looked from her mother to her dad.

"Well, we've got guests coming for lunch," Ron explained.

As usual, Twila didn't hesitate to speak her mind. "I thought we were having a family lunch."

"We are," Ron answered. "We are having a family lunch." For a moment the three stood there. On the drive over from church, Ron mentioned to Emily he might not say anything and just let it be a surprise, but looking at the puzzled expression on Twila's face, he thought better of his plan. "Twila, what would you think if we told you that Andrew and his parents are going to walk through the door in a minute?"

"What?"

Ron waited a moment, giving her time to comprehend a little of his question before he repeated it. "What would you do if we told you that Andrew and his parents ..." Before Ron could finish his question, Twila's face burst with joy and she rushed from the table toward the door as John and JoAnn entered. Ron and Emily followed and watched as Andrew's parents unselfishly released their son into Twila's hungry arms and Andrew so readily settled into them.

At the table they all talked and laughed and cried. Joey had to leave before the rest to head back to Oklahoma. The others remained, pushing their food around, unable to eat. "We've had movers at the house for two days and there are boxes all over but you will come over to the house, won't you?" Emily asked.

As soon as they all entered the house, Emily said, "Twila, in the basement storage room is the box marked, Grandma Toys. You know, the ones we've collected for so long."

"Wait a minute." Ron had reached to move a box from a chair in the living room. "What's this, Em?"

"Well now, how did that box get up here?" Emily took it from Ron and sat on the floor in front of Andrew. "I just guess the Lord arranged to have these up here and waiting just for you."

Twila lived her dream of two mornings earlier as she sat on the floor and Andrew crawled to her.

Although John had to be back in St. Louis for work the next morning, the Taylors seemed eager to stay for church that evening.

After the opening song of the evening, Dr. Herrod stepped onto the podium and shared a few opening remarks, then he spoke of the events of his day. "... Many of you know what our Twila went through more than a year ago when her baby was born. We haven't seen that child until his parents brought him here for our last Sunday." Ron motioned for them to come forward along with Emily and Twila. "This is John and JoAnn and Andrew Michael ..." Ron's voice broke and applause filled the auditorium. When it was quiet again, he continued.

"I don't know that anyone has ever given us a greater gift than John and JoAnn gave us today, other than the Lord giving us Jesus Christ. They didn't have to do it, but they did it because the Lord led them to. God bless you for it. I love you for it."

After they took their seats again, Ron signaled for Twila to come forward. "My daughter has never sung in public. I don't know that she's ever sung in private, but because of what God has done in her life, she has a special song."

As taped music filled the long, white-columned auditorium, Twila took the mike in her hands. A hush settled over the congregation as her sweet, untrained voice floated through the sanctuary. Only a slight tremor revealed the emotion she felt as she sang the simple melody recently released by Larnelle Harris.

Each person present identified momentarily with Twila's song; the miles of pain and crying; the loneliness and dying. Twila's eyes were closed as she sang of the blows and wounds, yet a warm glow spread across her smiling face as she shared the truth of her healing ... and came to realize Jesus was in it after all.

Twila presently lives with her parents, Dr. and Mrs. Ron Herrod, in Oak Ridge, Tennessee where she works part time and attends the local community college.

Seeing Andrew Michael is always a joy for Twila and each time confirms in her mind and heart that she made the right decision for them both when she placed him for adoption.

Ron and Emily delight in being grandparents and remain grateful for the continued, unselfish spirit of the Taylors to share Andrew. They've all become part of the Herrod family and brought with them unmeasurable peace and healing.

Both Ron and Emily have had the privilege of speaking in numerous churches and to other groups. Because of the burden of the Herrods for women in crisis situations, Women's Crisis Centers have been opened in Ft. Smith, Arkansas and also in Oak Ridge, Tennessee.

At the time of adoption, JoAnn immediately resigned her position, and now enjoys being a full-time mother and homemaker. Neither she nor John have ever felt threatened by the Herrods. They both feel that being chosen by God to be Andrew's parents has restored their sense of worth and value.

The agency, through mutual friends, did discover the families have met and maintain contact; therefore the agency decided to prevent the Taylors from any further possibility of adopting through Hope Agency or through other agencies in their networking system.

"It was really tough to accept their decision," JoAnn admits, "because we still want more children. But for Andrew and the Herrods, it's worth it. After all, when God speaks, we'd better listen."

D avid and Dawn (Herrod) Gibson have again joined her family in ministry and they serve together at Central Baptist Church in Oak Ridge, Tennessee. They are in the process of adopting and anticipate welcoming a baby into their home by May, 1992. "To see how the Lord led us in adopting out with one daughter and adopting in with the other daughter," Ron explains, "makes a great parallel of our spiritual adoption into the family of God."

Joey continues to live and work in Oklahoma City, Oklahoma. He freely admits his joy at seeing his family happy again but also questions the long term effects of the open relationship between the two families.

It's a question neither family can fully answer, nor do they feel it's a relationship advisable for every situation. The question they ask more frequently is, doesn't every child, adopted or otherwise, have hurdles to overcome, and won't they be better equipped to meet those hurdles when reared in a godly home with all the love and security of their entire Christian family?

Please send me:

When Evil Strikes by Lila Wold Shelburne. Despite seemingly impossible circumstances, Romans 8:28 is validated in this powerful story that reads like fiction.

_____ Copies at $9.95 = _____

Guilty Until Proven Innocent by Keith Barnhart with Lila Shelburne. Dramatic account of the prosecution of an innocent pastor charged with sexual child abuse. A must book for all who work with children. 1991 BOOK OF THE YEAR, *Cornerstone*

_____ Copies at $9.95 = _____

In His Steps Today by Marti Hefley. The novel that asks the question "What would Jesus do if he were living today?" A best seller that is fiction with a challenge.

_____ Copies at $7.95 = _____

Making the Most of the Best of Your Life by Kathryn Grant with Penny Giesbrecht. Gives fresh insights into dealing with the challenges of life that are faced by women of all ages.

_____ Copies at $9.95 = _____

We Can Change Americe ... and here's how by Darylann Whitemarsh. For Christians who want to change the direction our country is going. Step-by-step instructions and illustrations that are geared to the individiual.

_____ Copies at $9.95 = _____

12 + Me by Pat Likes. "Pike County Patsie" relives her years as the youngest of 13 children on a river-bottom farm across from Hannibal, MO. A warm, true story in the tradition of Mark Twain.

_____ Copies at $7.95 = _____

Please add $2.00 postage and handling for first book, plus .50 for each additional book.

Shipping & Handling _____

MO residents add sales tax _____

TOTAL ENCLOSED (Check or money order)_____

Name _____

Address _____

City_____State____Zip _____Phone_____

MAIL TO HANNIBAL BOOKS, 921 Center, Hannibal, MO 63401.
Satisfaction guaranteed. Call 1-800-747-0738 for quantity prices.